T5-AQA-354

The Big Book of
Miniature Horses

**Everything You Need to Know to
Buy, Care for, Train, Show, Breed,
and Enjoy a Miniature Horse**

KENDRA GALE

T
TRAFALGAR SQUARE
North Pomfret, Vermont

First published in 2017 by
Trafalgar Square Books
North Pomfret, Vermont 05053

Copyright © 2017 Kendra Gale

All rights reserved. No part of this book may be reproduced, by any means, without written permission of the publisher, except by a reviewer quoting brief excerpts for a review in a magazine, newspaper, or website.

Disclaimer of Liability
The author and publisher shall have neither liability nor responsibility to any person or entity with respect to any loss or damage caused or alleged to be caused directly or indirectly by the information contained in this book. While the book is as accurate as the author can make it, there may be errors, omissions, and inaccuracies.

Trafalgar Square Books encourages the use of approved safety helmets in all equestrian sports and activities.

Library of Congress Cataloging-in-Publication Data
Names: Gale, Kendra, 1980- author.
Title: The big book of miniature horses : everything you need to know to buy,
    care for, train, show, breed, and enjoy a miniature horse / Kendra Gale.
Description: North Pomfret, Vermont : Trafalgar Square Books, 2017. |
    Includes index.
Identifiers: LCCN 2017011384 (print) | LCCN 2017027076 (ebook) | ISBN
    9781570768521 | ISBN 9781570768200 (pbk.)
Subjects: LCSH: Miniature horses.
Classification: LCC SF293.M56 (ebook) | LCC SF293.M56 G35 2017 (print) | DDC
    636.1/09--dc23
LC record available at https://lccn.loc.gov/2017011384

All photographs by Kendra Gale except the following: 1.2 Michael Gale, 2.3 C Jennifer Jacula, 2.7 Michael Gale, 2.8 Michael Gale, 3.7 A Christine Tilleman, 4.11 B Jennifer Jacula, 5.8 ABC Jennifer Jacula, 7.9 AB courtesy of Crystal Lee, 7.11 AB courtesy of Christine Tilleman, 9.1 Michael Gale, 9.15 Michael Gale, 9.17 ABC Michael Gale, 9.18 ABC Michael Gale, 9.19 Michael Gale, 9.21 Michael Gale, 10.2 B Michael Gale, 10.3 Michael Gale, 10.10 Michael Gale, 10.11 Michael Gale, 10.18 Michael Gale, 11.6 Rick Kroll, 11.8 Rick Kroll, 11.9 A Rick Kroll , 12.1 AB Charlene Gale, 12.2 Michael Gale, 12.4 Michael Gale, 12.15 Rick Kroll, 12.16 A Michael Gale, 13.5 Charlene Gale, 14.6 ABD Charlene Gale

Book design by Lauryl Eddlemon
Cover design by RM Didier
Typeface: Optima

Printed in China

10 9 8 7 6 5 4 3 2 1

For Grandma and Grandad

CONTENTS

Acknowledgments

I really wanted this book to be a collaboration as much as possible, and I am so grateful to everyone who contributed in any way, especially my local Alberta Miniature Horse community! While it would be impossible to individually mention everyone who helped me with this project, a few thanks are absolutely necessary:

Dr. Crystal Lee for proofreading and checking my veterinary facts, as well as the whole staff of Burwash Equine Services for their support and knowledge—and I don't just mean on this project!

Jennifer Jacula and Charity Canty for being my first readers and helping me think of anything I'd missed covering.

Kathleen Winfield for proofreading the carriage driving information.

Peter and Terry Holt, and the staff and residents of Shepherd's Care Kensington, for allowing me to share their excellent programs. And to Peter and Terry for sharing Thumbelina and Bernadette's stories, and for Hollyhock Meadow, which is always my favorite place to visit!

Julia Morgan for introducing me to her amazing program and being so enthusiastic about this project.

Kimberley Locke and Bunanza for being the perfect clipping models.

Sherry Wilson McEwen and Dr. Lee for letting me photograph Scout's prepurchase exam on the coldest day of the year.

My neighbor, Rick Kroll, who heard about this project and immediately dropped off a disc of amazing Miniature Horse photos!

My brother, Michael Gale, for taking lots of weird pictures for me ("I need one of somebody painting feet.")

Christine Tilleman for brainstorming and story-sharing.

And, of course, Grandma, Grandad, Mom, Dad, John, Mike, Carrie, and my whole extended family for endless support and encouragement for all my Miniature Horse adventures!

PART 1:

Miniature Horse
Basics

Chapter 1:
The Horse for Everyone

1.1 Five-year-old Ethan leads Jerome, working together as a team!

1.2 The author and her horse Finnegan, waiting in line for the ribbon presentation after a fun Roadster championship class.

Why We Fall for a Tiny Horse

Miniature Horses are almost universally appealing, their small size attracting the attention of all ages. Anytime Miniatures Horses are at a public event, they're easy to find; just look for the crowd of people. Even beyond their small size, they win hearts wherever they go. When you factor in their larger-than-life personality and full-sized athletic ability, it's easy to see why so many people fall for such a small horse (fig. 1.1).

For Kids

Kids and Miniature Horses just fit. These horses are particularly appealing to children and can make a child's first equine experience much less intimidating. Where some children might be cautious approaching a 15-hand horse, very few hesitate to approach a Miniature. Science is only just beginning to prove the benefits of young people interacting with horses, though those of us who were lucky enough to grow up with horses already know it to be true, and the size of the horse has no bearing on the life skills he can teach. Good horsemanship learned with Miniature Horses is universal, so they are ideal to set young children up for a lifetime of horse love and learning—enjoyment through adulthood (fig.1.2).

Not Just for Kids

There are many reasons why adults find their way to Miniature Horses. Maybe they are lifetime horse people who, due to physical limitations, can no longer participate in riding activities. Perhaps they have always been a horse lover but never had the opportunity, and Miniature Horses give them access to the horse world for the first time in their lives. Or it could be that they simply fell in love with the most diminutive type of horse and everything that they can do (figs.1.3 & 1.4).

What Is a Miniature Horse?

A Miniature Horse is a "height" breed. This means that unlike many breeds of horses that are purebred regardless of the characteristics of the offspring, Miniature Horses must remain under a height limit to maintain their registered status. While most registries also require that they are from registered parents, there is usually a "hardship" option where an unregistered horse that meets the height limit can be registered for a fee,

"My parents purchased our first three Miniature Horses at an auction on my seventh birthday. I had been asking for a horse, and my mom was much more comfortable with small horses than big ones. We quickly entered the world of showing and driving, and three horses became over thirty. Some of my best and most important friendships growing up were made through our local miniature horse club. These friendships and my experiences with miniature horses inspired my eventual career choice to be an equine veterinarian."

Dr. Crystal Lee, Burwash Equine Services

provided he passes the inspection and other requirements.

Not every Miniature Horse is registered, however, and the term is one used quite generously with any very small horse. It isn't uncommon to find small ponies up to 10 hands under the moniker Miniature Horse. Ideally, a Miniature Horse

1.3 Miniature foal Gambler, therapy horse in training owned by Duane Kary, visiting with residents at Shepard's Care Kensington.

1.4 Hawk the Miniature Horse visits Hackney/Welsh Pony Dolly and Clydesdale Jamie.

should have the proportions of a full-sized horse. If you took a photo without any perspective, a correctly conformed horse shouldn't look obviously small, and you might be fooled into thinking he is 15 hands high.

Ancient History

The earliest ancestors of the horse, the diminutive, three-toed Eohippus, would make today's Miniature Horses look big. Standing just 18 inches at the shoulder, only a Miniature foal would look him in the eye. Evolution and many thousands of years brought us the tall and imposing horses we have today, but modern Miniature Horses have taken the opposite path—their size diminishing through careful breeding and many generations.

Miniature Horses have appeared in history for hundreds of years, with the earliest records tracing back to the 1600s. Performing in traveling circuses to the delight of audiences, being billed in sideshows as "The Smallest Horse in the World," or as a playmate for the children of a nobleman, Miniatures appear as novelties throughout modern history.

From Royalty to Pit Ponies

Later, Miniature Horses were recruited to work for a living. Bred specifically for use in the coal

"After my doctor suggested I give up riding (dressage) due to a back problem, I picked a breed I wouldn't be tempted to ride—the Miniature."

**Sherry Wilson McEwen,
Carousel Miniatures**

mines, they needed to be small enough to fit into the lowest underground tunnels, with the strength to pull a full load of coal back to the surface. Strength, durability, and work ethic were very important at this stage of their history, and it was the introduction of very small pit ponies that helped stop the use of child labor in the coal mines.

Pit ponies often lived their whole lives in the mines, as they found it was less stressful for them to stay in the dim underground light than it was to readjust to the bright sunlight above ground. It was said that the pit ponies were treated better than the miners as they were harder to replace. They formed close bonds with the men they worked with, with stories of ponies guiding their handlers out of the mine to safety. When I was a little girl, I had an opportunity to meet a very elderly retired pit pony in the mines of England. Now part of a tour about the history of the mine, the blind pony still lived in the underground mine he had worked in, and loved meeting his adoring public and begging sugar cubes.

Out of the Mines

In North America, the Appalachian coal mines began to move to mechanized mining and phased out their pit ponies in the 1950s. As the ponies were being sold off, some enterprising breeders went around and purchased all of the smallest for their own breeding programs. This was the beginning of the modern Miniature Horse in North America. Initially, the horses were bred exclusively for small size, with little regard to conformation or genetic deformities such as dwarfism, but with the advent of the registries the quality of the horses began to improve by leaps and bounds. The introduction of blood from other breeds of small ponies and horses, as well as generations of careful breeding, have created today's Miniature Horse, which, at its best, is truly a horse in miniature.

Height

The American Miniature Horse Association allows the registration of Miniature Horses up to 34 inches in height, as measured to the last hairs of the mane. The American Miniature Horse Registry has a division that allows horses up to 38 inches in height. Both registries require that horses must be from registered parents in addition to the height restrictions. While there is no worldwide standard for Miniature Horses, 34 and 38 inches tend to be the two limits most often used.

Registry Information

Perhaps due in part to the relatively short history of the breed, there are a number of Miniature Horse registries out there. The two largest and the most prominent in North America are the AMHA (American Miniature Horse Association) and AMHR (American Miniature Horse Registry).

American Miniature Horse Association
According to its website (www.amha.org), the American Miniature Horse Association is the world's leading Miniature Horse registry with over 200,000 horses registered and more than 10,000 members in 38 countries and provinces.

Founded in 1978, the AMHA promotes the breeding, use, and perpetuation of a standard of equine excellence in miniature,

How to Measure a Miniature Horse

Most horses are measured at the top of the withers, but Miniature Horses are traditionally measured to the last hairs of the mane, instead. The exception is when you are competing in an open-show or carriage-driving competition with other breeds. In these cases, you need to go by your horse's wither measurement.

To measure your Miniature Horse, first stand him on a level surface. Make sure that his feet are standing squarely, not stretched or hunched under themselves, as oddly placed feet can skew your measurement (1.5).

To find the last hairs of the mane, gently pluck the hairs in the vicinity; body hair will usually come out quite easily, while mane hair is more firmly attached.

Ensure that your measuring stick is completely vertical, and that the measuring arm is completely horizontal. This can be a challenge and is likely to be the biggest reason for disparity. Use of a bubble or spirit level can help.

Measuring a horse is not an exact science. If you are uncertain, measure a few times in succession: you will likely come up with an average or consensus measurement that you will feel is quite accurate.

1.5 For accurate measurement, horses must be standing square on a level surface.

American Miniature Horse Association

separate and apart from ponies and other small equines. Horses registered with the AMHA must meet the Association standard of perfection and cannot exceed 34 inches in height at the withers as measured from the last hairs of the mane (fig. 1.6).

American Miniature Horse Registry

Affiliated with the American Shetland Pony Club, the American Miniature Horse Registry's website (www.shetlandminiature.com) states that they

are the original registry for the Miniature Horse in the United States. Registering

1.7 American Miniature
Horse Registry.

as many as 10,000 horses each year and hosting an annual national show, AMHR recognizes two sizes and is the most comprehensive small equine option.

Division "A" Miniatures are up to 34 inches in height, while the Division "B" Miniatures are between 34 inches and 38 inches tall. Miniature Horses come in a full spectrum of coat colorings and patterns and (unlike Shetlands) a spotted appaloosa is an accepted and popular coloring in the American Miniature Horse Registry (fig. 1.7).

Many people raise double-registered horses, so they have the option to show in both major registries.

Other Miniature Horse Registries

There are other registries that register Miniature Horses, and whether they are applicable to your situation will depend on your location and interest. The Falabella Miniature Horse Association (www.falabellafmha.com) registers horses with bloodlines tracing to the original Argentinian Falabellas. The Pinto Horse Association of America

"My dad was getting into his seventies. He always had driving horses. My mom was worried that he would get hurt in some way and did not want him to have horses any longer. I heard about Miniature Horses and we went and bought two. I have had them ever since."

Sheila Cook, Double C Miniatures

1.8 A–C Depending where you live, there are a number of registries and organizations that oversee Miniature Horse activities.

(www.pinto.org) allows the registration of pinto Miniature Horses and offers classes and awards at many of their shows, including their World Show. The British Miniature Horse Society (www.bmhs. co.uk) and Australian Miniature Horse Association (amhs.com.au) register and oversee Miniature Horse activities in their countries, and similar registries and organizations are found throughout the world. Research what is available in your area, and if you wish to show your horses, find which registry sanctions the shows in your area (figs. 1.8 A–C).

Sport Organizations

If you are interested in combined driving or pleasure driving with your Miniature Horse, you may want to join the sport organization that oversees those events, such as the American Driving Society (americandrivingsociety.org). If you are interested in horse agility, then the International Horse Agility Club (www.thehorseagilityclub.com) is the one to join. Sport organizations not only keep you apprised of upcoming events, clinics, and news in the sport, but membership often also qualifies you for awards within the organization (fig. 1.9 A–C).

"I wanted to get into Combined Driving but found a regular horse and horse-sized carriage too much to handle on my own (for example, size of carriage, needing a bigger trailer and truck to haul it)…I was the person who thought Miniature Horses were cute, but what the heck were they good for. Then Kendra Gale and her Miniature Horse Hawk showed me that they can be true sport horses. I haven't looked back since and wouldn't dream of driving anything else! My Miniature Horse Rowdy has made it possible for me to participate in a sport I love in a way that's feasible for me to do on my own. I have never had so much fun with a horse!"

Tamara Chmilar

Local Clubs

1.10 *Your local club can be a valuable resource for education and networking.*

Local clubs are usually, but not always, associated with a registry or overseeing sport organization. A local Miniature Horse club can be a great resource to ensure you are kept in the loop for upcoming shows and educational events, as well a valuable tool for networking in your local Miniature Horse industry. Local clubs often do a lot of breed promotion at larger horse events and can be a great way to get to know other Miniature Horse lovers (fig. 1.10).

1.9 A & B *Sport organizations: International Horse Agility Club; American Driving Society.*

Is Registration Necessary?

If you wish to show your horse at shows sanctioned by the registries, you will need to have a registered horse. If this is not in your plans, while registration is a nice bonus from a traceability and marketing standpoint, it certainly isn't necessary, and is not a guarantee of quality. You can show your grade (unregistered) Miniature Horse in open shows, combined driving, and pleasure driving shows, and you can do all sorts of other activities with them, such as trail driving, horse agility, trick training, or pet therapy (fig. 1.11).

If your horse was registered in the past but his paperwork is out of date, with a little legwork and

"My co-worker at State Line Tack in Plaistow, New Hampshire, let me drive her mom's Miniature Horse, and I was hooked!"

Tina Silva, Crickhollow Farm

expense it is often possible to get it up to date. Contact the registry with what you know, and it will be happy to help get you on the right track and make sure you know everything you need to have to update his registration. Miniature Horses, because of their height restriction, are issued a temporary certificate of registration until they are three years of age, at which point you can apply for permanent status, provided they are still within the height limit. If they only have a temporary certificate and they are now 10 years old, their registration is no longer valid, but by paying a fee and filling out the correct paperwork you can get them up to date. Current paperwork is required to show your horse, or to register any offspring.

1.11 Ricco Suave, an unregistered, and once upon a time, wild and unhandled Miniature Horse is now an accomplished Combined Driving horse. While unregistered horses can't compete in sanctioned breed shows, there are lots of activities in which they can participate, and excel.

Chapter 2:

Coat Colors and Patterns

All the Colors in the Equine Rainbow

Equine coat colors are as varied and diverse as the breeds of horses, but nowhere else in the equine world do you find the full spectrum of color as in Miniature Horses. With no rules restricting color or markings as there are in many breeds, and unique combinations of color genetics rarely seen anywhere else in the horse world, breeding Miniature Horses is often surprising—and usually very colorful.

Color Testing

Sometimes, particularly if you are new to Miniature Horses and the unique combinations of colors they can express, it can be helpful to send in a hair sample for DNA testing of their color. There are several labs that provide this service at a reasonable cost. You can choose to do a complete color panel, or select just the gene(s) you are interested in or seem indicated. Color testing can also be beneficial when you are planning your breeding matches with a certain color outcome in mind, or you are standing a stallion at stud and this information may help mare owners decide if your stallion is the right cross for their mares. Horses that are lab tested homozygous for the tobiano color pattern, for instance, will pass on that gene to 100 percent of their foals, which will be very appealing for those who prefer pintos.

While most color testing is for more aesthetic considerations, if you have any suspicion that your breeding stock may carry the Lethal White Overo (LWO) gene, then you need to test prior to breeding. One copy of the LWO gene can result in splashy pinto markings. Two copies result in a solid white foal born without a properly developed digestive tract that dies painfully within 24 hours of birth. Since a 25 percent chance of a lethal foal isn't what anyone wants, horses that are LWO positive must only be bred to horses that are negative. The LWO gene can be as minimally expressed as a facial marking or a blue eye, so testing every single horse bred to a LWO positive is necessary.

The following is a brief overview of colors, modifiers, and patterns commonly seen in Miniature Horses. A proper, in-depth look at color genetics is a book topic all its own.

Base Colors

Black/Bay/Chestnut

The base colors of every horse, and all the diverse combinations seen in Miniature Horses, are *black, bay,* and *chestnut.*

2.1 A rich red chestnut, Lombards Redi to Be Royal Canadian ("Riot") owned by Sherry Wilson McEwen.

2.2 JEM Sir Lance Alot ("Lance") shows a bright gold palomino coloring. Lance is owned by Mary Ann Bartkewich.

The base color of each horse is determined by their Red/Black allele, genetically noted as e for red, and E for black.

Chestnut is a red horse, sometimes called sorrel but genetically the same color (fig. 2.1). Chestnut is recessive, genetically described as ee. Every horse, without any of the other modifiers, is chestnut.

"I bought the prettiest little blue roan mare that was also registered. I just couldn't stop myself and actually paid a lot for her. I never got a foal from her and she turned out to be the boss of all the big horses in the pasture but the underdog in the Miniature Horse pasture! At that point, I had only yearned for a Miniature Horse by looking at them as we passed by, so she was very special."

Linda and Peter Spahr, Hanlin Farm Miniatures

A black horse can be heterozygous (Ee—one copy of red and one copy of black) or homozygous (EE—where both copies are black). A homozygous black will never throw a chestnut-base foal, only black or bay.

A bay horse is a black horse with the dominant Agouti gene. The Agouti gene concentrates the black pigment in the mane, tail, and the points—lower limbs, muzzle, and ears—leaving the body varying shades of reddish brown.

Modifiers

A modifier acts on the base color to change it in some way, lighten, darken, or concentrate pigment.

Cream

The Cream gene dilutes the base color. A chestnut becomes palomino, a bay becomes buckskin, and a black becomes smoky black (fig. 2.2). If homozygous, the effect is intensified and a palomino becomes a cremello, a buckskin becomes a perlino, and a smoky black becomes a smoky cream.

Silver

Silver is another dilution gene, one that is rare in the horse world in general, but very common in Miniature Horses. The silver gene affects black pigment most strongly, so the expression of silver is greatest in a black horse.

A silver black is commonly referred to as a silver dapple, or in various breeds and parts of the world, as taffy or chocolate. These horses have coats that range from light silvery grey to dark steel grey or chocolate brown, with a lightened mane and tail, varying from just a shade lighter than their body color, all the way to snowy white (figs. 2.3 A–C). Despite the commonly used name of silver dapple, black horses with the silver gene don't always have dapples, though they can be very strongly expressed as well.

In a bay horse, the silver dilution is much stronger on the hair that would be otherwise black. Manes and tails are lightened from dark flaxen to white depending on the expression of the gene, and legs are generally a smoky or chocolate color.

A chestnut horse, which has no black pigment,

2.3 A–C Silver black comes in many varying shades: Vista Valley Wings of Glory, driven by Amelie Baker (A). Circle J Hawk, driven by the author (B). Ricco Suave, owned by Brenda Glowinski (C).

won't express the silver gene at all. This means the gene can "hide" until passed onto a foal with a black or bay base when it will be expressed again.

A horse that is homozygous for silver doesn't increase his expression of the gene, but it does predispose him to genetically linked eye issues. While a homozygous silver will pass on the silver gene to 100 percent of his offspring (with the associated eye problems), it is worth serious consideration prior to breeding silver to silver.

Dun

The dun markings are sometimes called "primitive" markings because they are commonly seen in prehistoric breeds such as Przewalski's Horse. The body color is diluted slightly, while the mane and tail are darkened, with a prominent dorsal stripe down the middle of their back, a cross over the withers and down the shoulders, and sometimes bars or "zebra stripes" on the legs.

As with silver, a homozygous dun doesn't increase the expression of the gene, but will mean every offspring of that horse will also be a dun. Colors include grulla, bay dun, red dun, buckskin dun, and dunalino.

Roan

Roan horses (blue roan, bay roan, red roan, buckskin roan) have white hairs mixed with their base color everywhere except their lower limbs, head, mane, and tail, which will stay their base color (fig. 2.4). Unlike dilution modifiers that change the color of every hair, the body hair of a roan horse will be 50 percent the base color of the horse, and 50 percent white.

Champagne

The Champagne gene dilutes the base color of the coat to a golden, creamy color, including every hair on the body. Champagne horses (including classic champagne, amber champagne, gold champagne) usually have light amber-colored eyes, and a pink skin with darker freckling.

Patterns

Pinto

Pinto markings are large white patterns on the body of the horse, alternating with the base color (fig. 2.5). Pinto genes can be minimally or maximally expressed, from horses with little or no body white to those who are nearly completely white.

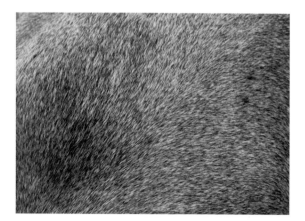

2.4 Roan is a mixture of white hairs with the dark hairs of the base color—in this case, black, to create a blue roan.

2.5 Circle J Sinatra, silver bay tobiano with two blue eyes, owned by the author.

2.6 *Rocky Mountains Razzle Dazzle and Circle J Unforgettable, minimally expressed buckskin tobianos, owned by the author.*

Tobiano markings are generally quite regular and even, with white markings on legs and head as would commonly be seen on a solid-colored horse. These horses often have dark patches over the flanks and chest, and can be predominately white or dark depending on the expression of the gene. Minimally marked tobianos can masquerade as solid-colored horses and surprise breeders with pinto offspring (fig. 2.6).

Horses that are homozygous for tobiano will pass on the gene to all of their offspring, a great asset if you are trying to breed for pinto markings.

Overo horses have white markings that are generally quite irregular with ragged edges. They often have one or more dark legs, and white rarely crosses their back. Usually horses with the Overo gene have distinctive face markings with lots of white (fig. 2.7).

2.7 *Erica's X Marks The Spot, a bay overo stallion owned by Craig Cline, shows the distinctive and unique facial markings associated with overo patterns.*

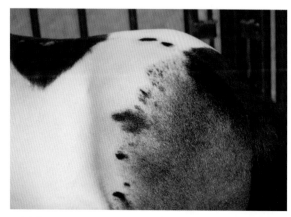

2.8 Sabino can create unique markings, like this roan patch on the hip of Diamond B Paddington, owned by Taylor Gibbons.

All horses that display the visual overo pattern are heterozygous, as it is lethal in its homozygous form (Lethal White Overo) (see p. 9).

Sabino is most easily described by thinking of a Clydesdale (like the horses in the Budweiser commercials). With big white socks, white faces, often a large belly spot and roan hairs throughout their coat, Clydesdales are a classic expression of sabino. Blue eyes, random patches of roaning that appear as the horse matures (particularly in

"Totally an impulse buy! I love Appaloosa horses. I never thought of owning a stumpy little Miniature Horse (I thought). Then I saw a five-day-old Miniature colt, liver with white blanket and spots. He was very refined and horse-like. He changed my whole view of Miniature Horses. I bought him on the spot. Best buy I ever made, never regretted it for a moment."

Joyce Ebert, R.V.T., Walking Bear Farm Miniature Performance Horses and Training Center

combination with tobiano), and jagged or mottled markings can all be expressions of sabino (fig. 2.8).

A maximum expression of sabino is a pure white horse, or sometimes nearly pure white, with a little bit of color on an ear. A minimal expression could be a sock, a blue eye, or a roan crescent on a hip or shoulder. While you can color test your horse for sabino, not all the sabino genes are testable at this time.

There are many different combinations and variations of the pinto genes, creating a wide range of expressions.

Appaloosa

Responsible for white markings on Appaloosa horses, the *LP (Leopard Complex) gene* is characterized by mottled skin on the muzzle, eyes, and perineum, as well as progressive roaning as the horse ages. The LP gene can have range of expression—from no visual signs at all to extreme white patterning. The expression of spotting in horses with LP will vary depending on influence of other genes, including PATN1.

All horses that are homozygous for LP will have congenital stationary night blindness, which is the inability to see in darkness or low light conditions.

PATN1 (Appaloosa Pattern 1) is associated with increased white in horses with LP. In horses heterozygous for LP, PATN1 will most often result in a leopard or near-leopard pattern. Horses homozygous for LP with PATN1 usually result in a few spot or near-few spot pattern. In order for high levels of white spotting to be visible on horses with PATN1, they must also carry LP.

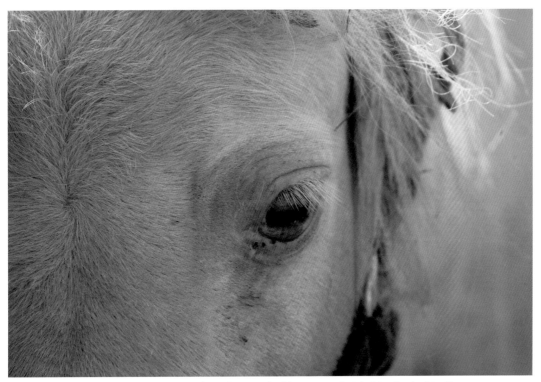

2.9 Thumbelina, owned by Hollyhock Meadow, showing the blue eyes and pink skin of a double dilute.

Mix N' Match

The genes we've just discussed can work in combination with another. You might have a base color of bay, with a cream gene so the horse is buckskin, and a silver gene to make him a silver buckskin, and a roan gene to make a silver buckskin roan, and a tobiano gene to make him a silver buckskin roan tobiano, and an LP gene so now he's a silver buckskin roan pintaloosa. And if that same horse had two copies of the cream gene, making him a silver perlino buckskin roan pintaloosa, then chances are he would be phenotypically (visually) white and you would have little indication about the full genetic smorgasbord

hiding behind that double dilute, and testing or resulting offspring would be the only way to illuminate it (fig. 2.9).

Many people start to think that Miniature Horses don't follow any of the established genetic color "rules" but it's just that there are so many genes potentially involved that you might not be able to easily see everything that is at play.

Foaling with Miniature Horses is never boring; there are so many options you are rarely completely sure what color your new baby will come out sporting. Even then, as he ages and sheds that foal coat, he might still have some surprises for you.

Chapter 3:
Choosing a Horse

First, Make a List

Buying a horse is always exciting, but especially so when it's your first foray into Miniature Horses. Too often, though, you hear how peoples' first horse just wasn't what they needed. Almost immediately, they have to buy a different one, or a second horse, or even sometimes get so discouraged by starting with the wrong horse that they give up on the idea altogether.

Before you even start looking, really take some time to think about your goals. What are you hoping to do with the horse? What is your budget? Do you have experience with horses? Every question you ask will help you determine exactly what you are looking for.

Taking the time to find the right horse, rather than the first one you see, will save you time, money, and heartbreak.

It is easy to fall in love with a Miniature Horse, and when you're horse shopping, falling in love can easily get you into trouble. Making yourself an actual, physical list of requirements will clarify exactly what you are looking for and help prevent you from jumping into the wrong situation (fig. 3.1).

Are you new to horses? Chances are you don't want to start with a youngster without any previous handling, or a broodmare due to foal soon. Want to show your horse at sanctioned shows? Then registration is a requirement, and you'll need to do a little research and find out which registries have the most sanctioned shows in your area.

Primary Requirements

Once you know what your goals are, you can figure out your most concrete requirements. These will vary depending on your goals:

• Want a show horse? Registration is going to be non-negotiable.

3.1 Making yourself an actual priority list can help you narrow down just what you are looking for in a Miniature Horse.

- Looking for your first driving horse? Lots of good experience in harness should be first on your list.
- Want to do therapy work? Temperament and handling experience will be most important.

Figure out your non-negotiable requirements and stick to them. The good news is that you should be able to get an idea of whether or not the horse is the appropriate age, has the experience and temperament, and is registered by asking the right questions before you ever meet the horse, thus minimizing the chances of falling in love with one that isn't the best fit for you.

It Would Be Nice If ...

Once your primary requirements are looked after, you can start looking at other things you'd like to complete the picture of your ideal horse.

Think you might like to learn to drive one day, but it's not a priority right now? Then "broke to drive" would be a big bonus, even if it isn't on your list of "must haves."

Always had a fondness for a certain color or pattern? This is where that consideration belongs—a good horse is never a bad color, so unless you can find every one of your primary requirements, the color shouldn't be a consideration. This doesn't mean that you can't get everything you want, just that you need to prioritize so that you don't end up compromising on the wrong thing.

Don't Fall In Love—Yet

It's so easy to fall in love once you meet the horse you've been thinking about. And sure, you want a horse that you're crazy about. But falling in love with a horse that isn't going to work for what you

"I was bitten by the driving bug and bought a Miniature Horse and cart to learn. I have now driven all types of horses and ponies but none more fun than a Miniature!"

Carole Moss

want to do with him isn't going to help you achieve your goals. If your budget is unlimited, and you can offer that horse a great home for the foreseeable future, then I take it back: go ahead and fall! But for most of us, this is not feasible, so keeping your heart out of the picture as long as possible can save you quite a bit of money and heartbreak.

The first thing you can do is run all your primary requirements and secondary wishes past the seller before you ever meet the horse. Then, even if the smoking deal is hard to resist, you'll know immediately that it is not what you're looking for before you go any further.

Remember to be true to your goals. Sometimes it helps to bring friends along, especially one with horse experience, but failing that, one with a healthy voice of reason. Not only can they weigh in on the decision, they also don't have a vested interest and are able to be a little more objective.

Purchase Price is the Cheap Part

Years ago, back when I was in high school, my best friend's family purchased an older driving mare from us for $500. Her dad loves to tell people that I cost him three-quarters-of-a-million dollars—he is counting, of course, not just the horse, but the equipment, truck and trailer, future horses, farrier bills, veterinary care, new acreage, new barn, and more—everything that came along over the years as a result of the whole "horse" adventure.

Buying the horse really is the most affordable part, and it costs the same to care for a $500 horse as it does a $5,000 horse or a $15,000 horse. Obviously, your budget will be an important factor, but choosing the "cheap" horse just because of the purchase price—especially when you are inexperienced with horses—can end up being much more expensive in the long run.

Alternatively, spending more money doesn't mean you'll automatically "get what you pay for": horses are emotionally priced, not logically. When you buy a car or a new appliance, there's a concrete reason why one model is worth more than another. Features, size, quality—all are quantifiable and easily assigned a dollar value. Horses aren't like that, and often people are happy to spend more to purchase their dream, and what they hope the horse will accomplish, which explains why an unproven yearling may fetch more money than an experienced driving horse.

Spending a bit more to get a horse from a reputable breeder instead of the auction mart is nearly always a good investment. Spending a small fortune for a well-promoted horse from a hot bloodline is less of a guarantee on your investment. Training, conditioning, grooming, and skill will all have a huge impact on what the horse achieves, regardless of how much you paid for him. Spending more doesn't mean an automatic winner.

Where to Look

Once you have your list of "needs" and "wants" figured out, it's time to start looking. This is the fun part! Horse shopping is exciting, and it means you get to look at lots of pretty ponies along the way.

Breeders

Probably one of the best places to start is with a simple Google search for nearby breeders (fig. 3.2). Not only will it give you an idea of what's available in your area, but breeders are good contacts to have. Even if they don't have what you are looking for, most breeders are happy to help point you in the right direction, or keep you in mind in case they see the perfect horse for you in their travels (fig. 3.2).

Pros

A reputable breeder can become your mentor as you move forward in your Miniature Horse adventure. Purchasing from a breeder means that you'll know your horse's medical and care history, training, bloodline, and everything else. A breeder may offer incentives such as paying your show fees (if that is one of your goals for the horse) or just be

3.2 A Google search is a great place to start, giving you a list of local breeders to check out.

3.3 Spend time visiting breeders and their horses: it can be a valuable learning experience, even if you don't find your new horse. Here, mares and foals play in the pasture at Circle J Miniatures.

a friendly face to answer questions. A good relationship with the breeder of your horse can also give you contacts for good veterinarians and farriers—it can be difficult to find a good farrier who is willing to work with a Miniature.

Good breeders also stand behind their horses. Often such horses come with a height guarantee (that is, should the horse outgrow his registration paperwork, the breeder will take the horse back) or a first right of refusal (if you ever sell the horse, the breeder will most likely buy it back). Even if it isn't outlined in the contract, reputable breeders want happy customers and a good home for the horses they raise, and they will usually work with you if it turns out the horse isn't right for you (fig. 3.3).

Cons

It can be tricky to figure out which breeders are reputable—that is, those who are interested in the betterment of the breed and concerned with the future of each foal they raise, versus those who are more interested in making a quick buck by selling cute little foals. Ask around if possible; see what experience others have had with a particular breeder.

The breeder that is offering the horse that checks all your boxes might not be local to you.

"I was not able to ride or show anymore. I was devastated for a while, but then I went to a show that had Miniature Horses driving, and I said to myself, 'I might be able to do that!' I drove my first Miniature that day and a month later, I had my own."

Nancy Balderston

But, buying a horse "sight unseen" is a risky move, and can involve a lot of added expense in shipping costs.

Things to Watch Out For

Ask lots of questions of the breeder, not just about the horse, but about management and health care, as well. A reputable breeder will generally be happy to share his program with you, and help you develop a similar system for your new addition. Any breeders who don't want to give you a tour to meet the rest of the herd, or act as though their management practices are a closely guarded secret should raise some red flags.

Double-check the paperwork on your new horse if registration is one of your primary requirements. Even reputable breeders can occasionally get behind on their paperwork, but if a horse is for sale as registered, they should have papers in hand and a signed transfer for you to register the horse in your name. Some breeders will even pay for the transfer of paperwork and provide the required photographs, but that is an "above and beyond" service that shouldn't be expected.

If you are not able to meet a breeder and see the herd, it's a great idea to ask for some local references to chat with. It still isn't going to be

"Remember they are horses and not just cute. If not trained well Miniature Horses will become pushy and hard to handle, and therefore, not too fun. Ask a lot of questions of people that have had Miniature Horses before you buy."

Nancy Balderston

a guarantee that you won't run into issues when your horse gets off the trailer, but any information you can get is helpful.

Auction

There is something exciting about an auction: bidding on your favorite horse, hoping the other bidders drop out before you reach your budget limit, the auctioneer shouting, "Sold!" and just like that, you have a new addition. The idea of finding a "diamond in the rough" for a great deal also has appeal, and keeps people coming back. But buying a horse at auction can be a risky endeavor.

There are two very different kinds of auctions where you can find Miniature Horses. First, and most common, is the general "small town auction," either included in an "Odd & Unusual" sale along with other small animals, or tacked on the end of a weekly horse sale. The second auction is a dedicated Miniature Horse sale, usually promoted and supported by breeders, with consignment requirements such as registration, vaccination, reserve prices, and a lot more pomp and circumstance.

Pros

Auctions give you a chance to see a large number of available horses all in one place and at one time. More formal sales will often have a previewing of each horse the day before the auction where you can drive a horse prior to sale time. This means you don't have to make a decision in a hurry when a horse first shows up in the ring. Many breeders' production sales are also broadcast online, so you can bid from the comfort of your own couch and arrange transport to bring your new horse to your door.

If you are a savvy horse shopper, not to mention a bit of a gambler, auctions are often a good place to pick up a bargain. If one of your considerations is that you want to give a home to a horse that needs one, an auction mart sale is a good place to find a horse to help.

Cons

In general, top quality horses aren't offered at auction, though there are exceptions (and the aforementioned "diamonds in the rough") at some breeder-supported auctions that have a higher caliber of horses. But it's a good idea to ask yourself, "Why is this horse being sold at auction?"

At an auction, you don't have time to consider your decision, and it's easy to get swept up in the excitement of a bidding war and spend way more than you intend for what might end up being the wrong horse.

Even if the horse you buy comes from a good home with detailed medical history and good general care, that doesn't mean the horse in the next pen has had the same experience. Always quarantine a horse that is bought from an auction to prevent transmitting a communicable disease to your herd at home.

Unscrupulous sellers will find it much easier to fool buyers at an auction where you don't have the time to really get to know the horse, or to double-check details such as registration. Heath and soundness issues can be easily hidden until it's too late and the deal is done. Some

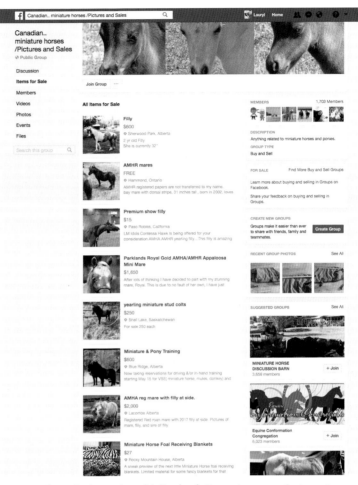

3.4 An online sale site, such as this Facebook Group, is a convenient way to see what's available.

people use an auction sale as a place to dispose of "problem" horses.

Online

In today's online world, the internet is probably the most common place to shop for a new horse to add to your family. Even if you're not actively searching for a horse, it's hard to resist a little casual online "window shopping" just to see what's out there. This is a risk-free, way of dipping your toe in the water in the very early stages of your Miniature Horse journey (fig. 3.4).

"As a long-time owner/rider/trainer of 'big' horses, I was intrigued with Miniature Horses when I first began hearing and reading about them around 1980. At the time I was raising my kids and not free to travel to where the breeders were, until one day a friend gave me a little booklet of Miniature Horse breeder ads. There was one within a half-day's drive—and the rest is history!"

Margo Cox-Townsend, Jess Miniature Horses

Pros

With almost unlimited selection and shopping you can do in your pajamas, it's no wonder shopping for horses online is so popular. You can easily see what's available in your area—and all around the world. If you are looking for a very specific horse, you can search beyond your local region until you find someone who has him.

The ability to readily communicate with breeders far from you, ask questions, and easily request more photos or a video makes online shopping the easiest way to find your new horse. Payment can be sent via e-transfer or Paypal,

"Research everything you can think of: hoof trimming, dental care, feed, shelter, overall health care, gelding, foaling. And most of all, figure out how to answer the question, 'What do you want to do with a Miniature Horse?'"

Theresa Lytle, Rocky Acres Miniature Horses

haulers can be organized, and your new horse can find his way to you with a minimum of time and effort on your part. Even if you don't purchase your horse online, it is a great way to research what's available.

Cons

First, there are serious risks to purchasing sight unseen. Even after reviewing current photos and videos, sometimes there are things you just can't see in a photograph. It is difficult to verify claims of movement, health, and training when working through a video, and hard to get a feel for the trustworthiness of a seller via email.

Unfortunately, online distance sales can sometimes be a way for less reputable sellers to get rid of a problem horse for a big chunk of money, knowing full well that the buyer isn't going to want to spring for additional funds to ship the horse back to them.

It can be particularly risky to buy a driving horse from a long distance: just because you have seen a video of the horse driving well, it doesn't mean that he is always that confident and well behaved, or appropriate for your level of skill.

Relying solely on the internet to shop for your new horse can cause to you miss out on some local gems. Some breeders have nice horses but do not have a website or don't have the time or tech savvy to consistently update it.

Buyer Beware

Just as with any group of people, most of those selling Miniature Horses are honest. They want a good home for their horses; consequently they want you to have all the information you need to decide if you'll be happy with a particular choice.

However, even a good seller might not realize that a horse isn't appropriate for you, so you must be aware of your own limitations. If you've never handled a horse before, you don't want to start with a two-year-old stallion that is going to challenge you at every step. If you're just learning to drive, you are much better off starting with a "Steady Eddie" with lots of miles, than a fire-breathing four-year-old roadster horse, no matter how pretty he is. Ending up with the wrong horse for your level of experience can become a nightmare.

There are always a few "bad apples" who can color your entire horse-buying experience. These are people who are only interested in making money, with no regard for where the horse ends up, or whether you are happy with your purchase. One go around with someone like this can really make you sour on sellers, and understandably so, even though there are absolutely more good ones than bad ones.

When you know the right questions to ask, you can help protect yourself from some of the common pitfalls.

Registered (or Not)

If you plan to show at sanctioned Miniature Horse shows, it is important your new horse is registered with the organization that oversees the shows in your area. In North America, shows are mainly sanctioned by either the AMHA or AMHR. Even if you don't show but would like to be able to resell or sell offspring to the show market, registration is important.

Check that the registration paperwork is up to date. Miniature Horses are issued a temporary registration certificate until they are three years of age and then, if they meet the height requirements,

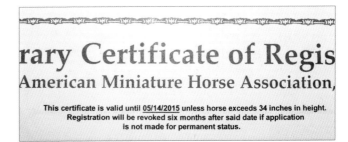

This certificate is valid until 05/14/2015 unless horse exceeds 34 inches in height. Registration will be revoked six months after said date if application is not made for permanent status.

3.5 Temporary registration certificates have an expiry date. When that date is passed, your horse's papers are no longer valid until renewed.

they are issued a permanent certificate. Each time the horse changes ownership, the new owner's name must be notated on his paperwork. Gelded status also needs to be reflected. Most of these things can usually be fixed if papers become out of date, but it can take quite an investment of time and money to straighten out (fig. 3.5).

Don't just purchase a horse advertised as "registered" and assume you are good to go. It might not be for the registry that you require—and, papers can also no longer be valid.

Bite

Your Miniature Horse should have an even bite, with top and bottom front teeth meeting each

"Get a Miniature Horse that suits the personality and the experience level of the person that will be handling it. If you have no intention of showing, registration papers are not a big deal. Seek the advice of a trainer or someone already involved in Miniatures as the care and upkeep are slightly different from that of big horses."

Kelly Wagar, Eldorina Equine

3.6 A *Thumbelina's underbite is severe as a symptom of her dwarfism, her lower teeth protruding far forward of her upper teeth, visible even when her mouth is closed. A bite that is even off by half the width of the tooth is considered a fault in the show ring, and can affect the horse's dentition.*

3.6 B *A correct bite should have the top and bottom teeth meeting evenly.*

"Learn all you can about horse behavior, communication, training, and care. Then treat your Miniature Horse the same as you would a 17-hand Warmblood!"

Tamara Chmilar

other and not being over- or undershot. An "off" bite is not only a serious fault for a breeding animal in the show ring—a trait you do not want to pass on to future generations—it can also set your horse up for ongoing dental issues that can continue to be a concern and require additional veterinary care for his entire life.

Check the bite on any horse you look at, and ask for a photo of the teeth of any horse you are investigating long distance (figs. 3.6 A & B).

Soundness

While it is pertinent to confirm the soundness of your potential new horse when you are looking for a performance prospect, it is always important to check for soundness, even if you are purchasing a breeding or therapy horse. You never want to buy a horse with an unknown lameness that will cost you time and money in your efforts to make him comfortable.

A pre-purchase exam performed by an equine veterinarian is the best way to confirm the soundness of a horse (see related discussion, p. 27). Issues can come to light that are unknown even to the current owner. In addition to performing a complete soundness exam, the veterinarian will give an overview of the horse's overall health as well as make an evaluation of his temperament throughout the exam and give a recommendation of suitability.

A pre-purchase exam costs a few hundred dollars, which is money well spent when you are purchasing an expensive horse from some distance, or even when you are spending less and don't want to be disappointed with your purchase. Even an inexpensive horse can cause significant veterinary costs when there is an underlying issue you're unaware of when you bring the horse home.

If you are not going to have a pre-purchase exam, be sure to watch the horse trot on firm ground, and, if you don't have the knowledge to recognize lameness, bring a more experienced person with you to watch the horse move.

Testicles

There should be two. Whether you are purchasing the horse as a stallion prospect or as a future gelding, you need to know. Cryptorchidism is not uncommon in Miniature Horses, and stallions with retained testicles need to be gelded, both for their own health and to prevent passing the issue on to their progeny.

The surgery to remove a retained testicle is much more involved than a standard castration, and has a corresponding increase in cost, risk, and recovery time. This isn't to say that you should automatically pass on a horse that requires cryptorchid surgery, but you will need to reevaluate your purchase budget for the added expense of the surgery.

It is a very unpleasant surprise to discover only one descended testicle after you already have the horse home, when you were expecting a future breeding stallion, or anticipating a routine, much more affordable, castration surgery. It is an important question to ask.

Height

When possible, measure the horse yourself prior to purchase. When purchasing sight unseen, it is going to be tricky to double-check the height, so is something you're likely going to have to take on faith.

Height is also going to be a risk anytime you purchase a young horse that hasn't finished growing yet. When it comes to a height breed

"Talk with as many Miniature Horse owners as possible, and look at lots of different horses. Go to Miniature Horse events. Then you need to know and be honest with yourself in what it is you want to do with the horse as that is extremely important in picking the right horse for yourself. Will he be just a lawn ornament or a rescue animal? Do you want a registered animal to compete in sanctioned shows? Do you want to show it in halter or performance, or do you want an all-round horse? Do you wish to do CDE or horse agility, or use him as a therapy horse? Do you have the time or experience to train your horse or do you need to buy an already trained horse? Every horse has a purpose but not every horse can do all things."

Pip Breckon

like a Miniature Horse, where their registration and show career requires them to stay within the limit, height is always going to be your biggest purchase risk.

Some young horses are sold with a height guarantee: if they grow too tall for the height limit of their registry, the seller will re-purchase or replace. In this case, you won't be out financially, but it is still heartbreaking once you've invested your time and energy in a horse to have him not turn out to be what you'd hoped.

Health

When you are able to see the horse in person, you'll be able to ascertain if the horse is in good health and weight, and review the environment he lives in and the general health of any herd mates.

3.7 A & B It can sometimes be hard to believe that the horse with a show clip in a professional photograph (A) is the same one standing in the pasture in his winter hair! (B)

When buying online or sight unseen, it is a lot more difficult to evaluate general condition, or decide if the horse is healthy enough to be shipped any distance. You can request current candid photos, and enquire about good health, but you will be relying on the honesty of the seller. A pre-purchase exam is the only way to properly evaluate the health of the horse when you are not able to see it for yourself.

When Photos Lie

Photos are a great tool for a seller. A great photo can make a horse look like a "million bucks" and encourage a buyer fall in love. But while a professional photo can enhance what's good, it can also hide the bad. Sometimes photos used for marketing purposes are photoshopped—edited to improve a horse's conformation. Or photos might be legitimate but were taken when the horse was a yearling, looking more refined and elegant than he is now.

Ask for *current* photos, making it clear that you understand they might not be as polished as the photos in their advertisement. Some sellers are very concerned you won't be able to look beyond the "winter woollies" thick coat, and they will lose a sale by sending candid photos. But the value to you of seeing the horse as he is now is likely to make you feel more comfortable about your choice, winter hair or not (figs. 3.7 A & B).

Other Questions to Ask

Depending on your plans for the horse, there are questions that become more—or less—important:

- How many foals has she had?
- Has she had any difficulty foaling?
- How much training has he had?

- Would you consider him a beginner-friendly horse?
- Has he been handled by children?
- How long has he been driving?
- What sort of driving experience does he have?

The more information you have about the horse, the more likely you are to be sure that this is the right horse for you. Good sellers, those who are truly concerned about finding the right place for their horse, are never reluctant to answer another question.

Another good one to ask is, "Why are you selling him?" It might simply be that the breeder can't keep all of them and this filly is related to their herd, or their other colt is a little taller so they're letting this one go. Or it might be that the horse has an issue that you aren't properly equipped to deal with. It never hurts to ask.

Vet Pre-Purchase Check

As I've mentioned, the best way to get an unbiased, professional opinion on a horse is to get a veterinary pre-purchase exam (fig. 3.8). Try to find

3.8 A qualified veterinarian's expertise is valuable in many aspects of horse ownership, and particularly when making a purchasing decision, a pre-purchase exam can help you make the right choice. Dr. Crystal Lee performs a flexion test on Circle J North Star to help her evaluate his soundness for new owner Sherry Wilson McEwen.

"Miniature Horses are NOT dogs."

Hilda Wilkins, Royal Mule Acres

an experienced equine vet in the area near the seller, but ideally not their usual vet; there can be a conflict of interest when a vet is working for you (a new client) and evaluating a horse belonging to a regular client. It is best for everyone when a different veterinarian is hired for the exam.

It is an extensive examination of the horse. The vet will check his heart, respiratory system, and his vision; listen to his gut sounds; get a detailed history from the current owner on any medical concerns; perform a complete lameness evaluation, including flexion tests; make detailed notes on any irregularities; and discuss any concerns with the horse's health, soundness, conformation, and temperament. If you'd like a more in-depth exam, routine X-rays of feet and joints can be performed.

It's also a good opportunity to obtain the full vaccination and deworming history so if all goes well and you move forward with the purchase, you can begin getting the horse onto your program. When you will need to transport the horse, a Coggins test (which must be negative), can be drawn at the same time. And when the vet has a concern, a blood test can check for the presence of anti-inflammatories or sedatives.

PART 2:

Care & Health

Chapter 4:

Working with Your New Horse

Horse Handling 101

It's important to dress appropriately around Miniature Horses. Although they are much smaller than their full-sized cousins, they're still strong and heavy. Never wear sandals or be in bare feet around horses of any size—if you value your toes! Wear sturdy footwear at all times.

Long pants are also strongly recommended as a horse rubbing himself can turn a simple halter buckle into quite a weapon on a bare leg. Gloves are good for leading or handling, as rope burn can occur following a simple spook, and it is very painful. Gloves are especially important when you are working with a fractious young horse, or working on a longe line or with the horse in long lines.

Leading

Horses are led from their left side. Use your right hand on the lead rope about 6 to 10 inches away from the halter and carry the rest of it in your left hand. Don't let the excess lead rope wrap around your hand; instead coil it back and forth so should the horse "take off," the rope will slip out of your grip rather than tighten around your hand. It's far better to have to capture a loose horse than it is to be pulled off your feet or break your hand. Remember, just because Miniature Horses are small, it doesn't mean they aren't strong and fast.

4.1 Ethan and Circle J Jerome show the proper safe leading position. They are working together as a team with a loose lead rope.

They are perfectly capable of inadvertently hurting you when you are careless.

Your horse should walk next to you, so you are positioned between his front legs and throatlatch. To ask your horse to step forward, use your right hand on the lead to push forward, offer a verbal cue, then walk yourself. You don't want to drag your horse: as soon as he begins moving, remove all pressure on the lead so that you are walking together as a team. Eventually, your horse should move off your body cues, with the lead rope there only as a back-up. Look where you want to go—not at your horse—as he is very aware of where your energy is focused (fig. 4.1).

Slow and Steady

When you need to work around your horse, remember that he is a) a flight animal and his first choice when startled is to run away, and b) he doesn't see the same way that you do. Even people who have never actually seen a horse in real life can tell you not to go behind a horse because you'll get kicked. But there is a little more to it than that, and there will be times that you need to go behind your horse. Remember, horses appreciate slow and deliberate movements, and while their vision is exceptional, which allows them to see almost all the way around themselves, they can't see directly behind. For this reason, they are more worried when a sudden loud noise or movement comes from their blind spot.

Horses don't want to kick you, and Miniature Horses tend to be even less likely to kick as a first choice—biting or rearing, these are the Miniature Horse's bad behaviors of choice! But when scared and not able to use flight as their first defense, they might kick. And yes, it will hurt. I once startled a yearling filly with her head in the feed pail

"Feeding needs to recognize the importance of enough proper forage in the diet, and also the need for any horse to not spend hours with an empty stomach. Slow feeding, frequent small meals, emphasis on forage, not so much grain, and recognition of the danger of laminitis/founder from an excess of grazing on lush green pastures in small equines is very important!"

Margo Cox-Townsend, Jess Miniature Horses

(I should've known better—I knew her back feet were on a hair trigger) and could feel the divot in my shin bone for years.

When your Miniature Horse knows it is you behind him, he is going to be far less likely to be frightened enough to kick. Always, approach slowly and talk to him; whenever possible walk up to his shoulder first, as that is where he can see you best of all, then keep your hand on him while you move to his opposite side.

Smarter, Not Stronger

When you are a complete horse rookie, I suggest some basic handling and horsemanship lessons to set you off on the right foot. Miniature Horses are horses in every way, and need to be treated as such. Disrespectful behavior isn't "cute" just because they are small, and they need to be held to the same standards of behavior as though they are 16 hands tall. Treat them like a horse, not a dog (fig. 4.2).

Their small size doesn't mean that you should ever attempt to overpower your Miniature Horse. First of all, you probably can't. He most likely

4.2 *Circle J Sir John Eh at a few weeks of age. Even though this behavior can be adorable when he's this little, it was immediately discouraged because it would quickly become dangerous as he grows.*

outweighs you, he's hugely strong for his size, and his low center of gravity makes him nearly impossible to budge when he doesn't want to move.

More importantly, every time you manhandle your horse rather than communicate with him, you're undermining your relationship and his confidence, and setting him up to develop even more undesirable behaviors as he attempts to defend himself. Find another way to explain it: use another technique; failing that, get experienced help.

Respect your Miniature Horse; never handle him roughly.

Feeding

To feed a small horse, it's important to look at the big picture. It's easy to get engrossed in all the available specialized feeds and supplements, or whatever your local winning trainer is feeding, but remember one thing: a Miniature Horse is still a horse.

Eats Like a Horse—Only Less

All the same rules that apply to the average 1,000-pound horse, still apply to a 250-pound horse (the weight of an average 34-inch Miniature Horse), just appropriately scaled down. This is where lots of people get into trouble. For example, if you've always fed your saddle horse three flakes of hay, twice a day, and your Miniature Horse comes along and you feed him one flake, your ratio still isn't quite right—a quarter of what your riding horse eats is a better starting point than a third.

Another issue with feeding horses is that inexact measurements, such as one "flake," as in the example above, or one "scoop," tend to be the common nomenclature and these are definitely not standardized units. I've had bales of hay where the skinny little flakes were perfect for a feeding for one Miniature Horse and bales where a single flake would've sufficiently fed three.

The general rule of feeding forage is that your horse needs to eat 2 percent of his body weight per day for maintenance, or less for weight loss, to a minimum of 1 percent. Note that is per day, not per feeding, so you are looking at an average of 1 percent per feeding. By that math, with your average 250-pound, 34-inch Miniature Horse, you are going to feed 1.25–2.5 pounds of forage twice a day, depending on whether the horse is in a weight-loss or weight-maintenance program (fig. 4.3).

Square-baled hay isn't the only option for forage: feeding from round bales; hay cubes; hay pellets; haylage; and pasture are all options depending on where you live, but the feed-by-weight rule still applies. He needs need to eat at least 2 percent of his body weight in forage each day.

How Evolution Made Them Eat

Forage is very important beyond simply being a nutrition source. Horses evolved to live in a harsh environment, where they had to travel great distances and consume a large amount of poor quality forage. They would naturally graze for 18 hours a day, so their digestive tract depends on there always being new forage available for digestion. Humans, by contrast, have evolved to eat when food is available—in meals. As a result,

4.3 Despite their common use, the terms "flake" and "scoop" are not a standard unit of measurement. It is far better to feed your horse by weight.

our stomachs produce stomach acid for digestion only in response to food. Horses, on the other hand, produce stomach acid all the time, in anticipation of that constant supply of forage that their evolution relied upon (fig. 4.4). Their teeth have

4.4 Horses—even Miniature Horses—are grazing animals, with a physiological need to eat for most of the day.

4.5 *With high quality feeds and busy schedules, most horse owners feed their horses at "meal times."*

developed specifically for constant chewing of rough fiber. Their adult teeth continue to erupt throughout their lives as the crown of the tooth is ground down by constant chewing.

Despite their unique small size, a Miniature Horse is still a horse, and these evolutionary truths apply to them just as they do to their much larger cousins.

How We Made Them Eat

Our management of horses generally isn't in line with the way horses evolved to eat. Instead of full-time access to low-quality forage that takes lots of chewing and requires lots of feed to cover nutritional requirements, we provide them with high-quality forage and extruded feeds specially developed to include everything required by the horse. Instead of allowing them to eat all day, we feed our horses in meals for our convenience and their health; we certainly don't want them to have free-choice access to the optimal nutrition that is available to them. In many ways, this is much better—diets are balanced to keep horses healthy with specialized feed for every type and athletic use (fig. 4.5).

But remember all that stomach acid? The horse's digestive tract doesn't get the memo that it is getting everything it needs in those two meals a day, and it just keeps producing stomach acid, looking for something to digest. When it doesn't have food, it starts eating away at the lining of the stomach, and those lesions are known as "gastric ulcers." It is thought that as many as 90 percent of performance horses have some degree of ulcers at a point in their careers, and Miniature Horses are no exception.

Less Isn't Always More

Miniature Horses are often what is termed "easy keepers," and there is an impression that they get "fat on air" because you can feed them so little. But this isn't true of all Miniature Horses and it's important to feed each horse as an individual. While most people new to them tend to overfeed, occasionally you find someone who says they were told to feed just a "handful" of hay, and a poor, ribby, underweight horse is the result. In addition, by decreasing the amount of forage too much, even when the nutritional differences are made up in concentrates (grain, extruded feeds, supplements), you are dramatically increasing the risk of gastric ulcers.

The Dangers of "Winter Woolies"

It is recommended to closely monitor your horse's body condition so you can catch any required changes to your feeding program early and make adjustments before your horse becomes too fat or too thin. Miniature Horses present their owner with a unique challenge—as compared to their larger counterparts—and that is their winter hair. Miniatures grow a very impressive winter coat, and they grow it early and keep it late, often even in climates where such a thick coat isn't necessary for warmth (fig. 4.6). This fur is a great asset for keeping them warm, but it can hide a multitude of "sins," so it is important during the winter months

4.6 Miniature Horses are well suited to outdoor life, even in cold climates.

"Feed for what each horse needs. Some are super easy keepers, some are not. My horses eat almost the same year round, a little more energy food for the workers come spring. That way their nutrition stays the same all year. I find cubes better nutrition with less simple sugars than local hay, so I feed a lot of cubes and only a bit of long-stem hay (in nets with tiny holes)."

Joan McNaughton

to actually put your hands on your horse on a regular basis to monitor his body condition. If you rely on a visual assessment, you might miss some serious issues that will need attention.

Weanlings, especially, grow a very thick wooly coat, and they are among the most vulnerable to losing weight during their first winter. Elderly horses, as well, should be carefully monitored, but any horse can have a health or dental issue and suddenly lose weight, so feeling routinely

4.7 Since they grow impressive winter coats, it is very important to regularly put your hands on your horse to feel for body condition.

4.8 Slow-feed hay nets are an excellent tool for feeding in a more natural way with a smaller amount of forage spread over a longer time than loose hay would provide.

for fat cover over ribs, hips, and backbone is very important for the winter health of your horse (fig. 4.7).

Feeding Naturally in an Unnatural Environment

So what can you do to help your horse stay healthy and happy? It's a bit of a quandary—you need to give him the nutrition he needs, but not allow him to get overweight, as this comes with its own health risks.

If your management system allows it, divide the same amount of feed into more meals (three or four instead of two). This lets the horse spend more of his day eating and less time fasting. Remember, it's during that fasting time that not only is he at an increased risk of gastric ulcers (discussed earlier in this chapter) but more likely to develop stereo-typical behaviors such as cribbing and windsuck-ing (chewing on fences, and biting onto objects

and gulping air into their bellies—a vice that can have serious health consequences).

A slow-feed net is a great tool you can use to help simulate that natural grazing experience. Slow-feed nets have small openings in the mesh, and instead of just being able to eat mouthful after mouthful of hay, the horse has to work each piece through the holes first. A variety of brands are available with different mesh sizes. A three-quarter-inch net is a good starting point, but some Miniatures may need to go to a half-inch net to really slow their eating down (fig. 4.8).

While it is recommended to initially provide your horse with loose hay in addition to using a net, horses usually adapt very quickly to it and tend to enjoy the challenge. You can get slow-feed nets in every size, from one feeding all the way up to a full round bale. The round-bale nets have the added benefits of virtually eliminating the usual wastage that occurs with traditional round-bale feeders, and greatly reduces the health concerns, which are an increased risk of heaves from inhaling the dust inside the bale, and eye injuries, again from horses standing with their head inside the bale while they eat.

Feeding for Show

Feeding a horse into show condition can be a bit different, particularly if you are feeding a halter horse. When looking for that "tucked-up" appearance, with lots of cover and fill over his topline, many bloodlines don't do well on a forage-only diet. You will have to play with what works well for your horse, but reducing the hay content of the diet and supplementing with beet pulp and extruded feeds can help get the appearance you are looking for. Be very cautious, however, about reducing the forage portion of their diet below 70 percent. This hay content, whether from loose hay, cubes, bagged hay, grass, or any other forage, is critical for the health of your horse.

Dangers of Whole Grains

If you are considering supplementation, look first to the extruded and complete feeds. These are commercial feeds that are formulated for specific requirements—for example, for young growing horses, hard-working, or senior horses. These extruded feeds are preferable to feeding the whole grains themselves (oats, corn, barley) because they are much more digestible, as well as being carefully balanced so the horse gets all necessary nutrients.

Whole grains, because they break down into sugars in the digestive tract, are risky for horses with metabolic issues (very common in Miniature Horses), and they set up an environment in the digestive tract that makes a horse more prone to

"Miniature Horses can subsist nicely on good quality hay, salt or mineral block, and clean water. Not too many of them require any kind of special feed. When showing I feed a soaked mixture of beet pulp, alfalfa pellets, and vitamins and minerals, as well as good quality hay free-choice."

Linda and Peter Spahr, Hanlin Farm Miniatures

both colic and ulcers. Whole grains are also more likely to make your horse "hot," with an excess of energy that makes him prone to difficult behavior as well as being more of a challenge to train—kind of like a toddler at Christmastime.

Forage (Again)

As mentioned, some sort of forage needs to be the backbone of your feed ration (fig. 4.9). Forage is critical for the horse's health, and in many cases,

4.9 Forage, in one of its forms, needs to be the largest part of your horse's diet. Shown here are a flake of grass hay, alfalfa/grass-mix hay cubes, and alfalfa pellets.

a horse won't require any additional nutrition. An appropriate amount of good quality forage, fed in a manner that allows the horse as close to a natural, grazing situation as possible, as well as access to salt and fresh water, is a good place to start any ration.

Grass Hay

Grass hay is probably the place to start when figuring out a ration. The type of grass will vary depending on your region. Where I live, the grass hay is primarily timothy. Its quality can vary dramatically, and while checking out color, smell, and cleanliness is a good policy, it tells you very little about its nutritional content. To be absolutely certain what you're feeding your horse, you need to test your hay and find the amounts of crude protein, digestible energy, and minerals so that you know how much to feed to get recommended daily values, and how much complete feed you need to supplement to make up any deficiencies. If you don't test your hay (and you're not an expert on balancing rations), carefully monitor any change in body condition

"Be ready to change your feeding regime as needed. Figuring out what works best for each Miniature Horse is practically an art form and science experiment combined! What works well for one horse may be a terrible diet for another. I monitor each of my Miniature Horses and ponies closely for weight and behavioral changes as well as how their manure looks."

Tina Silva, Crickhollow Farm

and adjust your feed ration accordingly. Miniature Horses can change their body condition very quickly. You'll generally see the results of any ration changes promptly.

Fescue is a type of grass hay generally a good feed for horses, but often susceptible to a fungus. When pregnant mares eat the fungus, they can develop serious issues such as prolonged gestation, premature separation of the placenta, a dysmature foal (a foal that is full term gestationally, but shows symptoms of a premature foal), and lack of milk production. If you have foals born on your facility, the best choice is to avoid fescue in your pastures and hay supply. Avoiding fescue entirely may not always be an option, and in those situations, broodmares are pulled off the fescue prior to the last 60 days of gestation.

Green feed, which is a cereal grain crop such as oats and barley, baled on the stalk, is a commonly used feed for cattle. It can be dangerous to feed to Miniature Horses due to its high grain content.

Straw is sometimes used as a supplementary feed to give the horse the chewing and stomach-filling requirements, especially during winter months. Straw should only be used if the horse is getting all his required nutrition from his hay or other feed, and he should be monitored carefully for colic and encouraged to keep up his water intake.

Alfalfa Hay

Alfalfa hay is a legume, different from the grass family of hays. Alfalfa is high in protein and can be too rich for many Miniature Horses unless fed in moderation. Horses that are overweight and prone to developing Equine Metabolic Syndrome (a form of insulin resistance) should avoid high percentages of alfalfa in their diet. A mixture of

grass and alfalfa hay can be a good mix for a Miniature Horse. My elderly horses, with various age-related issues, including PPID (equine Cushing's disease), do well on grass/alfalfa mix cubes.

Alfalfa is also high in calcium, which is beneficial for buffering stomach acid and prevention of gastric ulcers. Adding alfalfa to the diet of horses with a history of ulcers can be a good preventive measure.

Pasture

Many people discount pasture as a feed source for Miniature Horses, but as with all horses, grass is their natural diet. Again, the amount needs to be scaled down accordingly, but unless your horse has a metabolic concern that precludes him from the high sugar content of fresh grass, pasture can certainly be the bulk of his diet if managed appropriately (fig. 4.10). Not to mention, when you have access to a pasture, it's free feed!

Depending on the quality and amount of pasture, you'll want to restrict the time your horse has access. For example, in spring when the grass is lush, he'll get just two hours, increasing gradually to living on grass full time in the fall, and eating down pasture until the transition to hay in winter. With this in mind, developing your paddocks and pastures with a smaller pen to use as a dry lot that opens into a pasture makes turning your horses out and bringing them back in much less labor intensive.

Be aware that Miniature Horses, if given the opportunity, will eat every green thing available to them. So do check your pastures and paddocks for any plants or weeds that could be toxic, because once the grass is gone, they won't be very picky about what they eat. Since this list of such plants varies greatly from region to region, you'll need to

4.10 *Grass is appropriate forage for most Miniatures but access to it must be carefully managed. In spring and summer, they require significantly less grazing time to meet their nutritional requirement than in fall and winter.*

familiarize yourself with any plants in your horse's environment that may be of concern.

I routinely feed even my show horses a pasture-based diet, transitioning them to hay or cubes only in the week prior to the show so they are used to this new feed.

A

B

C

4.11 A–C There is no such thing as a "one-size-fits-all" feeding program. Broodmares, performance horses, and retirees all have very different nutritional requirements.

Cubes/Haylage/Pellets

When you are dealing with a show horse, these food items are both convenient and easy to digest. I also prefer cubes for my elderly horses as they often have teeth issues and a diet of soaked cubes prevents them from choking on improperly chewed feed, as well as ensuring they are keeping up their water intake.

Another benefit of more processed forms of forage is that you know exactly what is in them, with the nutritional information on the label. You also know that it is going to be of consistent quality, which isn't a guarantee with hay. Their downside is they are eaten faster than hay, again leaving your horse with a period of fasting.

Concentrates

Forage isn't always enough for every horse, and there are some situations where your default feeding program should include concentrates. Concentrates include all "hard" feed from extruded and complete feeds, to whole grains and mixes.

When and Why

Horses at different stages of life have different nutritional requirements. Young, growing horses (especially in their first year), lactating mares, and old horses all need additional nutrition, and the best option is always going to be a commercial complete feed specially formulated for the requirements of your horse. Horses in work, or any horse that is having difficulty maintaining condition, may also need supplemental feed (figs. 4.11 A–C).

Whenever you make a feed change—or an addition—do it gradually over the course of a week to 10 days in order to prevent a digestive upset or colic. The good news is that modern commercial extruded feeds are generally very safe and easy on horses' stomachs, though it is better to be safe than sorry. However, be aware that this is not the case with whole grains, and you should take great caution if you do decide to include oats or other cereal grains in your horse's diet—this includes rolled oats and mixtures such as sweet feed and COB (corn-oats-barley). Personally, I feel that the numerous risks involved in feeding whole grains are not worth it and I never feed anything but extruded feeds (fig. 4.12).

Feeding Your Horse as an Individual

When it comes to developing a feeding program, it can be easy to take people's well-meaning advice to heart, especially when it's something that works really well for them. But even if their horses look amazing on their feeding regimen, be sure to consider your management system and your horse's age and workload as well. For example, maybe a person has an amazing-looking horse that is competing in combined driving and being worked for a solid hour at least five days a week. It's more than likely that your pasture pet who goes for a walk to the mailbox with you every few days doesn't require the same diet!

It's important to monitor every horse individually. With the very high prevalence of metabolic issues, Miniature Horses are definitely more likely

"Limit grazing on green grass. Miniature Horses quickly become obese or (worse) can founder. My horses get quality grass hay and soaked beet pulp with Purina Miniature Horse & Pony Feed. All amounts are adjusted to whether in foal, nursing, weight, and work load."

Joyce Ebert, R.V.T., WalkingBear Farm Miniature Performance Horses and Training Center

4.12 With a wide variety of feeds available, horse owners no longer have to give oats or sweet feed. Instead, they can choose a feed specifically formulated for their horses' nutritional requirements. Note the salt blocks—a convenient way to allow access to salt—in the foreground.

to require a low sugar, low starch diet, but occasionally there are "hard keepers" that simply need more nutrition to maintain their body condition.

Supplements

Horse people love their supplements. Ask everybody who feeds horses and they'll be happy to tout the benefits of whatever supplement they choose to feed. Flip through any magazine and you'll find pages of advertisements, promising everything from joint health to improved temperament. But what does your horse really need?

Salt

While humans are often told to reduce their sodium intake, horses don't have this problem of too much salt in their diet. Instead, you need to supplement their sodium. Ensuring horses have full-time access to a salt block allows them to self-regulate their salt intake, and in most cases this is sufficient. Hard-working horses, or sometimes elderly ones, can benefit from loose salt added directly to their ration. Plain table salt will do, at a rate of 1–2 teaspoons per day for a Miniature Horse. In the winter, especially during cold snaps, I make a special effort to add salt to the rations of my older horses to be sure they get all the sodium they need and to encourage them to continue to drink lots of water.

4.13 Feed supplements for horses are a booming business.

"Learn all you can because every horse has different needs, and sometimes it takes experimentation to find what works best for a given horse. With some Miniatures, it takes creative ways to ensure the horse can fulfill their need to eat continually throughout the day. Good quality forage is always my number one priority."

Tamara Chmilar

Vitamins and Minerals

The essential major minerals are: calcium, phosphorus, magnesium, sodium, chloride, potassium, and sulfur. The essential trace minerals needed are: iron, zinc, copper, selenium, manganese, iodine, and cobalt.

Generally, horses on pasture have a sufficient level of these minerals (depending on your location—for example, our pasture is low in selenium), and most commercial feeds are balanced to include the minerals and vitamins needed for optimal nutrition. For horses not on pasture or a complete feed, there are vitamin/mineral supplements available. Check with your local feed store and your veterinarian to determine which one is right for your horse.

Specialty Supplements

There are an amazing number of feed supplements available. No matter what you feel your horse needs help with, be it a respiratory issue, coat conditioning, hoof health, temperament, or basically anything else, there is a supplement for it. While the efficacy of them vary, generally supplements don't do any harm (except perhaps to your bank account) and they might be just what your horse needs (fig. 4.13).

Water—In All Weather

Water and forage are the two most critical elements to keep your horse healthy and happy. Horses need to have unlimited access to water to keep their digestive tract working properly. The number one killer of horses is colic, and lack of hydration can be a major contributor.

Encouraging your horse to drink in extreme cold and extreme heat is especially important. During the winter, it is very important to understand that horses *cannot* get enough fluid from eating snow, and must always have access to fresh, thawed water. If you are in a climate where you routinely get below-freezing temperatures, investing in a heated bucket, stock-tank heater, or automatically heated waterer will not only be beneficial for your horse's health, it makes your winter chores much less painful—no one likes spending time outside breaking ice.

When it's cold, horses drink more if their water is warm, while in hot weather, cool water encourages them to increase their intake. Keeping their water in a shady spot, or adding ice to the pail can help encourage your horse to stay hydrated in the heat.

Temperature swings can lead to an increased incidence of colic, and reduced water intake is likely a key factor. Everything you can do to encourage your horse to drink is going to be beneficial to his health.

"I feel like the best way to manage a Miniature Horse's food is for him to have a job that involves more than being cute in the yard! I take my training for shows seriously and see too many overweight horses out there. Some new horse owners may not even realize the many, many health risks of an overweight or obese horse. Instead of driving them mad by not feeding them they will be far happier being in a routine of regular exercise plus feed management."

Brenda Glowinski, Glowinski Miniature Horse Supplies

Chapter 5:

Housing and Transportation

Housing

Miniature Horses are hardy and do best living in an outdoor environment. You definitely don't need to have a fancy, top-of-the-line facility in place before you bring one home. But you will need a safe place for him to live and somewhere for him to escape from the weather, be it the heat of the sun or bite of the wind. Even if your property already has infrastructure in place for horses, it will need to be carefully evaluated to ensure it is appropriate for Miniature Horses. There is a reason they have a reputation as "fence crawlers," and it is mostly because people assume the same fences that hold a 15-hand horse are appropriate for an 8-hand horse. Spoiler alert: They aren't!

If you intend to keep your horse at your home, check that your property is zoned for horses, as despite their small size, generally the same land requirements apply as for full-sized horses. If you intend to board your horse elsewhere, I strongly recommend finding a boarding facility prior to purchase because it can be a challenge to find one set up to accommodate Miniatures.

5.1 The safest fences (like this one) avoid gaps between the wire that small hooves could get caught in.

Fencing for Short Horses

Likely one of the biggest struggles for new Miniature Horse owners—particularly those who suddenly find themselves with one—is fencing. The traditional two- or three-board fence probably isn't the best option for keeping your horse safe, unless it is appropriately sized. Often the bottom board on a fence built for a full-sized horse is far too high. And if you have or plan to have foals, then your fencing needs to be even more secure (fig. 5.1).

5.2 *A solid wire fence with smaller gaps in the lower portion of the panel is a good option.*

A mesh horse fence, or page wire, is a good option, provided the openings aren't too large. Anything that a mini can squeeze his head through to get at fresh grass will be quickly stretched out of shape and become less and less likely to contain him.

"Hog panels" or solid wire mesh panels are a good option, particularly when they have smaller spaces toward the bottom of the panel. Everything you can possibly do to prevent a tiny hoof from getting caught in the fence needs to be done (fig. 5.2).

A good way to create a temporary pasture for rotational grazing, or to reinforce a less ideal fence, is by using electric fencing. Once or two "hot wires" can be run along the inside of a fence to prevent rubbing or fighting through the fence.

"Since it can get really hot at times here, and we also can have serious winters. I try to have shade for their water buckets in the summer, sun on them in the winter...although I do use heated buckets in the winter. I construct sun shades for the outside runs in the summer, for my Miniatures to stand under. My permanent run-in sheds are deep, front to back, and south-facing, and the ground slopes downhill from the open side (even though we don't have much rain!)"

**Margo Cox-Townsend,
Jess Miniature Horses, New Mexico**

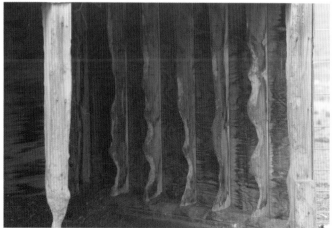

5.3 *Wood fencing is quite safe, but can be expensive to upkeep. Miniature Horses often fulfill their chewing requirements to the detriment of wooden structures.*

A mesh electric sheep fence or electric tape can allow you to temporarily fence a new space for grazing. Once horses understand the fence is electric, they'll generally be very respectful of it. Board fencing alone, particularly around a paddock without access to grazing, is often chewed through by bored horses, looking to satisfy their biological requirement for grazing (fig. 5.3).

No matter how safe you feel your fences are, horses are notorious for getting hurt, and you need to minimize the risk. The second day I turned my mares with their young foals out in a brand new, small mesh wire fenced pasture, I found the smallest filly with large rubbed raw spots on both shoulders. To this day, I have no idea how she hurt herself, as the fencing was as secure and safe as it could be. Imagine if she'd been in a less carefully fenced pasture!

Space to Play

While Miniature Horses are small, they do require enough space to be able to properly stretch their legs and play. How big your paddocks need to be will depend on your management system. If your horse is turned out into a larger pasture for daily grazing, then a smaller individual paddock is fine. If he is going to be kept in the paddock long-term, or you'd like to keep a number of horses together, then a larger paddock is necessary. Every paddock or pasture that your horse lives in needs to have a shelter, unless it's one that will be used only short-term and you are able to move him out of the weather, when necessary.

Our smallest paddocks are set up as long narrow pens, 10 feet wide and 60 feet long, with a shelter at one end and waterer at the other. This way the horses are able to race up and down the length of the pen and get lots of activity in the smaller space. This type of pen works well for one or two horses, and is a good solution for elderly horses that require special care and nutrition, mares with new foals, weanlings, stallions, or any other time you need to separate a horse or two from a larger herd.

When fencing your pastures, the bigger the better. Remember that you can always use temporary electric fencing to further divide the pasture for rotational grazing,

Shelter from the Storm

Miniature Horses generally adapt very well to cold weather, but do need to have access to shelter to get out of the wind and keep dry. In hot weather, shade becomes very important. Unless they have a lot of brush or tree cover in their pasture, you'll need to have a shelter. A basic three-sided shelter, large enough for your horses to share together peacefully, is sufficient. When you are in a cold climate, consider a low profile, such as a calf shelter, to allow the horses to keep it warmer without the dead space above them. If you are more concerned about the heat, an open shelter that gives shade but doesn't stop the breeze might be better.

Position your shelter so that it opens in the direction least likely to have howling winter wind blowing in—for example, our winds tend to come from the north or the west, so our shelters open to the south or southeast, with the added bonus of catching as much of the winter sun as possible (fig. 5.4).

Outside Is Best

While your horse does need to be able to get out of the weather, in a run-in shed as just outlined, he doesn't need to be locked in. Allowing him

"Limit rich spring pasture. If you are not showing, let your Miniature's coat grow in the winter and leave him outside, except in cold, wet, rainy times."

Carole Moss, Tennessee

to choose whether to be inside or outside is the best option. Often in the winter, my horses will be cheerfully pawing through the snow to find a delicious bit of last summer's grass, while the wind howls around them and the snow piles on their backs.

If your Miniature Horse has snow on his back, it's actually a good sign. It means his thick winter coat is doing its job, and insulating him effectively

5.4 A three-sided calf shelter makes a cozy space for Miniature Horses to get out of inclement weather. Frankie and Johnnie snuggle into their shelter and enjoy the sunshine, safely sheltered from the wind chill of more than negative 20 degrees Fahrenheit.

5.5 *When your Miniature Horse has snow on his back, it's a sign that his winter coat is doing its job not allowing body heat to escape and melt the snow.*

with no body heat escaping to melt the snow. Don't brush the snow off! It is also insulation, and disturbing it might make him wet, and a wet horse is a cold horse (fig. 5.5). Horses are meant to be outdoors, and for their physical and mental health, as much outside turnout as possible with your management system is best.

Note: If your shelter or barn is made of tin, be sure it is lined with plywood as a kick barrier. A kick could easily puncture through the tin, causing devastating, potentially life-ending wounds from the sharp edges.

Bringing a New Horse Home

When you're putting in fences (and you have a number of horses), it's a good idea to plan for a separate place for: quarantining your new horse, keeping a sick horse separate from the herd, allowing an individual to get a specialized feed, or separating a bully that just won't get along with the rest of the herd.

The safest way to introduce a new horse into your existing herd is *through* a sturdy fence. Allowing them to get to know each other this way—without having "full access"—will help to prevent any of them from getting hurt. Horses, being herd animals, can be very defensive against a newcomer.

Once the new horse has been living next door for a while and there is no longer any kicking or squealing through the fence, it works best to introduce the horse to one new friend first. The new horse will find integrating into the herd a lot easier if he already has a friend; he is less likely to be picked on when you add two horses to the herd, even if one of them is a long-time member that has only been removed for a short time.

Adding a horse to the herd causes some shuffling of the hierarchy, and there can be some pinned ears and chasing going on for a bit. Initially, watch them very closely; any sustained chasing, biting, kicking, or other violent behavior will require your intervention to prevent injury. Often, it can be helpful to remove the bully for a while until the new horse finds his place in the herd, and then try reintroducing them all again. Give the herd the largest space you have available so they can run and play, as well as get away from each other if they need to.

Similar to people who are just never going to

get along, sometimes you find horses whose personalities don't mesh. It is usually easier to have horses get along in a larger herd; there are enough of them so that each can find a friend. Smaller turnout situations can bring to light "inter-equine" problems that you didn't realize existed (figs. 5.6 A & B).

Stalling

There are times when a barn with a cozy stall comes in handy. For example, it's much easier to monitor a foaling mare overnight when she is under a camera, and in really bad weather, I like to keep my elderly horses inside overnight to ensure they don't get chilled. Many people like to stall their show horses for convenience and to be sure they get their individual diet. But if you do keep your horse inside, for whatever reason, it is critical that he gets as much turnout as possible. Constant stalling leads to the development of stereotypical behaviors like cribbing and weaving, and it contributes to health issues such as ulcers and colic.

5.6 A & B The safest way to introduce a new horse to your herd is through a fence (A), not turned right out together (B).

"Ireland can be extremely rainy during the winter months through to spring; it's very important that horses are kept as warm and dry as possible. Waterproof rugs/blankets are lifesavers and we usually bring our Miniature Horses in at night, too. If they are clipped they usually wear an extra rug under their outdoor rug when they are out and a heavy stable rug when they're in at night, and are fed hay throughout the day/night to keep them warm."

Meabh Breathnach, Oakwood Stables, Wicklow, Ireland

Stall Size

An average box stall for a full-sized horse is 10 or 12 feet square. For a Miniature, 6 or 8 feet is sufficient, though more space is good if stalling is going to be a big part of your management system. Stalls should have good ventilation, and when repurposing full-sized stalls, be sure that your horses can see out of the stall and observe other horses in the barn. It is very stressful for a horse to be isolated, so make sure that even when stalled he can have contact with others.

Flooring

Flooring in your stall can be, dirt, wood, or concrete, and each has its advantages and disadvantages. Concrete is going to be the easiest to clean and disinfect, but is the hardest on your horse's legs. If you have a cement floor, it should have rubber mats and deep bedding to provide cushion. Dirt floors are the easiest on your horse, but will wear away with time, get wet with urine, and

"The winters here can be very cold and the snow exceptionally deep. I have found that for the most part I don't have to blanket my guys unless I have taken them to the arena and they come home damp. They have a full bedded shelter that they use to keep out of the snow. When the snow gets too deep we plow out the pen for them as they can't pack it like big horses do. They have access to a heated waterer, which is perfect as well."

Kelly Wagar, Eldorina Equine, Redwater, Alberta, Canada

not keep your horse very clean when it's the day before a show.

There are a lot of different stall mats available, some with antibacterial properties and others with extra cushioning so they feel almost like walking on a pillow or mattress. If your horse is going to spend a lot of time in his stall, then looking into some of these more advanced—and pricy—options might be a good idea.

Bedding

Stalls need to be bedded to absorb urine and make a soft place for your horse to lie down. What you choose to use for bedding is up to you: straw is often the cheapest (though it can be hard to find in small, square bales), and it makes a warm comfortable bed. When foaling out a mare, straw is preferred because it won't stick to the wet newborn and risk getting into little eyes and nostrils. However, straw lacks absorbency and can be more difficult to clean as compared to other options.

Shavings are the most popular bedding. You can buy them bagged at your local feed store, and if you use lots of shavings, you can also have a bulk delivery to your farm. All wood shavings are not created equal, however, and you'll want to find a brand that you prefer: avoid dusty shavings and be aware that large chips are less absorbent and more difficult to clean. Shavings absorb urine very well, minimizing the harmful ammonia in your barn, and are very easy to clean using a stall fork to sift out wet and soiled bedding (figs. 5.7 A & B).

Other options include pelleted bedding that expands with contact with water and is very absorbent and easy to clean. Many people really like this option, while others feel it doesn't make

5.7 A & B Rubber mats, clean shavings, and the ability to see other barnmates make a comfortable stall.

a comfortable bed for their horse and use it as a base layer under shavings or straw instead. Shredded newspaper, sand, and peat moss are also sometimes used for bedding. It's a personal decision, and you can try out a few options before you find out what works best in your management system.

Maintenance

Stalls need to be kept clean for the horse's health and well-being. If he is in overnight, the stall needs to be cleaned daily. If, for some reason, he has to be inside full time (due to stall rest to heal

an injury or foaling, for example) then the stall needs to be cleaned at least twice a day. Remove all manure, as well as any wet or soiled bedding and add more fresh material as needed. Every so often, stalls will need to be stripped of all bedding, swept clean, and disinfected; I like to be sure and do this prior to foaling season each spring, and as needed throughout the year.

Outside shelters can also be bedded, as particularly in the winter, it's a good idea to give horses a warm dry space to lie down. Shelters often don't need to be cleaned as frequently as stalls, as horses can come and go, but if your horse tends to like to use his shelter as a "bathroom," then proper attention must be paid to keeping it clean and comfortable.

Your horse needs to have access to water anytime he is contained in a stall, and it must always be clean, fresh, and thawed. A simple pail hanging from the fence, rinsed and refilled on a regular basis, is fine, and a heated pail that plugs into an outlet will work well in an unheated barn in winter. There are automatic watering systems, as well.

Keep your stall well maintained, and check regularly for any damage that might cause a risk, such as a loose board or protruding nail.

"Canadian winters! We have lots of shelters, heated water buckets, and netted hay bales to keep our Miniature Horses happy."

Kaycee Lunde, Amaretto Miniature Horses, Airdrie, Alberta, Canada

Manure Management

You need to have a plan in place to deal with manure. Since both manure and bedding is compostable, a manure pile can be used to compost the waste, and then it can be spread on pastures. Manure should spend some time in a pile to let it age and allow parasites to die off before spreading.

Alternatively, manure can be hauled away. There are services that provide a dumpster and empty it, or haul your manure away for disposal or compost.

Transportation

One of the first things you'll need to address is how you are going to get your new Miniature Horse safely transported to his new home. And maybe your new Miniature Horse has company and you have bought more than one (we all know they're like potato chips, and you can't just have one)! After all, a horse is a herd animal and shouldn't be expected to live on his own.

The small size of Miniature Horses can both make transporting easier, or more complicated, depending on the situation. The good news is that miniatures tend to be much more willing to load into a trailer than a full-sized horse, by virtue both of their size-to-trailer ratio and natural bravery.

Horse Trailer
The safest way to haul your Miniature Horse is in a trailer built for livestock; whether horse or stock trailer, it is set up to be safe for live animals, with good ventilation, and sturdy construction.

If you have a horse trailer, it may need some modification. The standard dividers in horse trailers are at an awkward height for miniatures.

Smaller ones just walk underneath them, while bigger horses might get themselves wedged underneath. Unless your dividers are "stallion dividers," or go right to the floor, they need to be changed or removed. Some people tie or latch the dividers back out of the way so that the trailer is still available for hauling big horses. Horse-trailer dividers are generally easily removed, and you can have a Miniature Horse insert built that will slide into your trailer and attach safely with appropriately sized dividers. This way, when you decide to sell your trailer you can simply pull your Miniature Horse divider out, replace the horse-sized dividers and have a larger (no pun intended) resale market available to you, as well as your insert ready to pop into your new trailer.

While dividers are handy, they're not necessary. If you only plan to haul one or two horses, they can be tied without a divider, or ideally, hauled loose. Again, your management system and preferences will play a large part in what works well for you.

Modified Cargo Trailers

With their lower price point, some people choose instead to purchase a cargo trailer and convert it for use with Miniature Horses. If you go this route, you need to be aware that there are some serious safety concerns with it as compared to a purpose-built livestock trailer, and be prepared to do some legwork to make it a safe place.

Most cargo trailers are not suitable. Not made to carry a live animal, they don't have ventilation, which is critical for a horse's well-being during transport. You would need to install suitable vents to keep your horse breathing easily. The floor may also not be appropriate and require extra bracing and reinforcement so check the trailer is rated for

the weight you will be asking it to carry. A safe divider or stall to contain your horses will also need to be installed.

Carefully look into the costs involved in converting a cargo trailer. It could well be that a horse trailer would amount to a similar investment when you include all the modifications necessary, not to mention you can be sure it is appropriate for safely hauling livestock.

Unconventional Transport

Everyone has seen a picture of a "Mini Van" modified to haul "mini horses," and if you've been at all involved with Miniature Horses you've probably seen someone who hauled a horse in the back seat of a car or behind the seats in an SUV. By virtue of Miniature Horses' small size and accommodating nature, these unconventional horse transport options are possible.

But "possible" doesn't automatically mean that it's a good idea. Any of these options need to be evaluated, both for the safety of your horse, as well as the human passengers.

I have a large raised-roof modified camper van that I use to haul a Miniature Horse. My grandad built a sturdy standing stall for the horse, so that not only is the horse contained to keep him from "helping" the driver or otherwise bouncing around and causing issues, he is also secure in the case of an accident. If, heaven forbid, you are in a collision with your horse inside your vehicle, you want to do everything you can to prevent him from becoming a projectile, both for your horse's sake and for your own safety.

Miniature Horses also can be hauled in the back of a pickup truck with a cab, some of which are specially manufactured for the purpose. Again, you'll need to watch that there is

Miniature Tales
The Hawk's Nest

When I started competing in Combined Driving, with just my horse Hawk and me traveling to events, it didn't make sense to take the whole truck and trailer for one little horse, especially since I wasn't a confident trailer driver and would need to talk a family member into coming along anytime I wanted to go. I started shopping for a van, and when I found one my grandad helped me (or rather, I "helped" him) modify it for hauling Hawk. We pulled out all the camper infrastructure to give us more room and installed a standing stall securely to the frame of the van to keep Hawk safe. This left lots of room to load the cart, the panels to create a pen for Hawk when we reached our destination and everything else we needed for the journey (figs. 5.8 A–C).

When we got to a driving trial, I would set up Hawk's pen under the awning so he was out of the weather, or shaded from the sun, unload the cart to make more room, and set up an air mattress for me to sleep on for the weekend. Hawk, my Chihuahua, Timmy, and I had lots of fun adventures, giving the van the moniker, "The Hawk's Nest!"

While Hawk has retired from driving due to an injury, The Hawk's Nest still gets lots of use anytime I want to haul just one horse (or sometimes two). My new driving horse, Rocky, likes riding in the van even more than Hawk did and is always keen to jump in and go on another adventure. I love that I can very easily head out without the hassle of a trailer, not to mention still fit in a drive-thru to get myself a Diet Coke—you can't do that with a horse trailer!

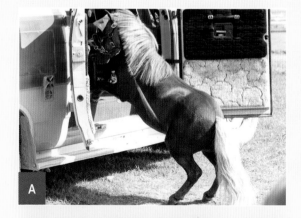

5.8 A–C While not a traditional way to haul livestock, "The Hawk's Nest" is a convenient and comfortable way for both horses and humans to travel.

sufficient ventilation and good footing, and that you've got a plan for getting your horse loaded and unloaded.

Because of the small size of Miniature Horses, you can certainly be creative in your method of transportation, but you do need to make careful preparations to keep both you and your horse safe.

Travel Tips

Transporting your horse, even in the most comfy and safe accommodations, is going to be stressful for him, and there are things you can do to make everything go as smoothly as possible.

Loading

Begin by teaching him to load ahead of time, and let him learn that the trailer is a good place to be. While chances are good that, with a little help, you could physically push, pull, and lift your Miniature Horse into a trailer, this is certainly not going to make it a pleasant experience and should be avoided.

Allow him to explore the trailer at his own pace, reward him for any movement toward the trailer at first, then every foot into the trailer. Let him hang out in it and eat cookies so he gets the idea that it's a fun place to be. Sometimes, it can help to lift a foot and place it into the trailer to give him the idea, and try it with or without a ramp if you have the option because some horses prefer a ramp while others would rather step up.

Taking a bit of time and teaching your horse to load easily and comfortably will pay off in the long run. Usually Miniature Horses catch on very quickly when given the chance to learn in a relaxed and positive environment.

Trailer Environment

One of the best ways that you can help make your horse's hauling experience a good one is to let him travel along with an experienced horse, one that will be very relaxed about trailer travel and give the new horse confidence.

Clean, dry bedding is a good choice to ensure your horse will have stable footing and fresh air during his trip. The exception is a hot environment with lots of open windows and vents. Blowing shavings can be hard on both horses' eyes and respiratory systems, and you might choose to haul in a clean trailer without bedding instead, and/or put a fly mask on your horse to help protect his eyes.

Horses are adept at injuring themselves in the trailer, and tall, padded shipping boots are available for Miniature Horses to protect their limbs from both trailer dividers and other horses. If you choose to use shipping boots or wraps on your horse, make sure they are properly applied and check on them frequently.

Depending on the temperature, you may also blanket your horse. As he won't be able to move around, when it is cold, you are responsible for keeping him warm. With everything else involved with traveling, you don't want the added stress of him catching a chill. Alternatively, trailers can be very hot and you don't want to automatically blanket your horse just because he is being trailered somewhere. Frequently check the ambient temperature in your trailer, feel under his blanket, and adjust ventilation and layers of blankets as needed to keep your horse comfortable.

Horses can travel loose, tied, or contained by a divider. If you tie your horse for traveling, particularly on long trips, ensure that he is able to drop his head. It is hard on his lungs and can

5.9 When you don't have dividers, a horse should be tied long enough to be able to comfortably move his head, but short enough so he can't get a leg over the lead—or get into other trouble.

predispose him to shipping-related illnesses when a horse can't drop his head and properly clear out his lungs and respiratory tract (fig. 5.9).

On a long trip, give your horse a net of hay so he can nibble on the way. Every time you introduce a stressful situation, the more roughage you can feed to keep his stomach full and happy will lower the risk of gastric ulcers.

Horses also need to be encouraged to drink regularly. Any time you stop to feed and water yourself (or use the bathroom) you should offer water to the horse. On long trips, the use of paste electrolytes can help encourage horses to keep drinking, or you can feed a mash of soaked feed (hay cubes, beet pulp, or complete feed) to help increase his water intake. Horses can be reluctant to drink on long trips, but lack of hydration predisposes them to colic, so everything you can do to keep him drinking is important.

There are cameras available to watch your horse in the trailer from the cab of your truck: you can check to see all is well in the back. Unless you do a lot of long hauling, this probably isn't necessary, but is a nice perk for your peace of mind. On shorter trips, check on the horses each time you stop.

Mechanical Maintenance

The trailer needs annual maintenance for checking brakes, floor, and wheel bearings. And double-check that your hauling vehicle is in good repair and is rated to pull the trailer. Every single trip, check and double-check the hitch and safety chains, and that your trailer lights are working. Every door should have a safety snap, latch, or lock to avoid accidentally opening, and doors must be rechecked every time you stop. Remember, you are responsible for the safety of your horse on the road, and you need to make sure everything that is in your control is as safe and secure as possible.

Chapter 6:

Grooming

Routine

Day-to-day grooming means a lot more than just keeping your horse clean and attractive. Proper grooming allows you to carefully examine your horse for an issue with his skin or legs, or injuries you might not otherwise notice. Time spent grooming is also a great opportunity for bonding, as grooming is a social activity. Rubbing or scratching places that itch will benefit your whole relationship.

An assortment of tools in your kit will make grooming easy for you and pleasant for your horse. A rubber curry comb allows you to loosen stuck-on mud and gives your horse a lovely scratch and massage. A dandy brush is stiff and takes dirt out of the coat, while a body brush is softer and removes dust and polishes the hair. Since Miniature Horses grow a lot of winter hair, you definitely need a shedding blade or another shedding tool to help with your springtime grooming. A hoof pick to clean out hooves and check for stones or thrush (a fungal or bacterial infection of the frog on the sole of the horse's hoof) is an important part of your routine, particularly *before* and *after* any sort of work to check that the feet have no issues that could cause soreness or lameness.

You also need detangling spray to make mane and tail grooming go more smoothly; and using a hairbrush-style brush is often more effective than a traditional mane comb, although a comb is better for separating sections for braiding. It is good idea to have some braiding elastics on hand as well—you may wish to braid the forelock so it doesn't get in the eyes or tangled in the bridle; band or braid the mane to convince it to lie on one side; and braid the tail to keep it up and out of the mud, or to encourage growth by protecting the long hairs from being snagged and pulled out.

To Clip or Not

It is a commonly held belief that Miniature Horses won't shed their coat on their own, so must be body clipped each spring. While in some cases,

"Give a good general grooming often enough to keep your Miniature Horse basically clean, while allowing you to be 'hands on' and able to notice any injuries/insults to the horse's physical being. Keep his feet cleaned and properly trimmed at all times and at proper intervals!"

Margo Cox-Townsend, Jess Miniature Horses

6.1 Because they grow more hair than an average light horse, Miniatures take longer to shed it out, but they will—with some time and elbow grease. Dazzle shows off a beautiful, slick, dappled summer coat.

owners clip their horses for show (Miniatures are nearly always shown in a full body clip—see the show section for more detailed information, p. 97) or comfort, or just because they want to, Miniatures certainly will shed out with a little elbow grease. Even yearlings, with their thick woolly coat, may take a little more time—but they will shed out. Sometimes a rough clip on a yearling can be less labor intensive than routine currying, but the extra handling of frequent grooming certainly isn't bad for a yearling (fig. 6.1).

Blanketing

Clipped Horse

If you do decide to clip, it becomes your job to keep your horse warm. Depending on the climate, this means blanketing at night, even in the summer. There are a wide variety of blankets available, from a flysheet designed to keep insects off without overheating a horse, to a heavy winter blanket and hood that can replace his natural coat in bad weather. A light sheet keeps a horse clean and helps to polish his coat before a show, and a fleece cooler wicks away moisture following exercise or a bath.

6.2 Usually, a Miniature in full winter coat doesn't need to be blanketed, even in extreme weather. However, 19-year-old Paco was shivering at the start of a sudden and prolonged cold snap; he became much more comfortable once he was blanketed.

Unclipped Horse

With their natural coat plus a good shelter from wind and weather, a Miniature Horse rarely needs to be blanketed. If his coat is dry and he can get out of the wind, then he usually does well in any sort of weather. Monitor him closely, however, as some horses, especially older ones, or those with health issues, may need a blanket to help them stay comfortable in inclement weather. Once you do decide to blanket, you'll need to be the one responsible for taking blankets on and off as needed to keep the horse comfortable, at least until you can have a stretch of weather warm enough for his coat to "fluff up" and restore the air space that is such an important part of his insulation (fig. 6.2).

Benefits of a Blanket

A blanket is helpful for older horses or those struggling to gain weight; they don't have to expend extra energy on keeping warm. Any time you have a blanketed horse, however, it is very important to regularly take the blanket off. From rubs to dramatic loss of condition, a blanket can hide a lot. It is not uncommon for an elderly horse to become dangerously underweight without his well-meaning owner being aware of it.

If you want a blanket to encourage shedding, it probably isn't going to be as effective as you'd like it to be without also adding additional light. Horses begin to shed with the lengthening daylight in the spring, so in order to convince them to shed out of season, you'll need to artificially lengthen their day by keeping them under lights long enough to fool them into thinking it's already summer. Just extend their day, but don't put them under lights for 24 hours a day.

"Keep your Miniature Horse dry in the winter—once wet, they seem to stay wet, and then the skin gets yucky. Body clipping in the late spring just makes them feel good—not a show clip, just get the long thick hair off and check that skin out. Elbow grease is better than all the store bought products! Lots of brushing and TLC."

Joan McNaughton

Blanket Fit

A blanket must fit well for safety and comfort. Straps should be adjusted so that they aren't too long, and I suggest you loop the hindquarter straps through each other to keep the blanket in place. Straps that are too long are a danger: a horse can catch a leg and hurt himself, while a blanket too tight can rub or create painful pressure sores. To be safe, whenever your horse is blanketed, it needs to be regularly removed for a thorough grooming, which gives you the chance to become aware of any issues before they become serious.

Mane and Tail Care

Miniature Horses are adept at growing hair, and manes and tails are no different with an over-abundance of both thickness and length. Regular care keeps it manageable and I find a hairbrush the best option for combing through thick manes and tails, with a good detangling product to make the job a lot easier. Miniature Horse manes are prone to "wind knots" (also known by more colorful names such as "fairy knots" and "witches' knots") and lots of detangler and patience is going to be the solution, using your fingers to pick just a few strands of hair free from the knot at a time (fig. 6.3).

Alternatively, some people like to roach (shave off) most of their Miniature Horse's manes. Be warned, however, that it specifies in the show rules that Miniature Horses are to be shown with "full mane and tail" so roaching is not going to be allowed in the show ring. Personally, I love their abundant manes and tails and like that I can encourage lots of mane growth in my horses that are not being shown.

In many cases, less is more when it comes to tail care. Keep in mind that it takes a long time to grow those long tail hairs, and each time you use a brush or comb, you are pulling out some more tail hairs. Some groomers recommend only using your fingers or a soft body brush to remove tangles from the tail. The gold standard in tail care is to braid a clean, dry tail, then bundle it up in a sock or bandage to keep the long hairs from being snagged and pulled out (figs. 6.4 A–D). If you want a long, "fairytale" tail that drags on the ground, this is the way to go. Be aware though, that by "putting the tail up" you are removing

6.3 *Long manes are prone to wind knots. Routine brushing prevents them from forming, but if you do need to deal with a wind knot, use lots of detangler, and carefully work a few strands of hair loose at a time. Much of the hair in the knot itself won't be attached, so once you've worked the mane hairs loose, you'll be left with a knot of hair.*

"I recommend Cowboy Magic® for the manes and tails, and Absorbine® ShowSheen® after a bath, particularly on any white parts."

Carole Moss

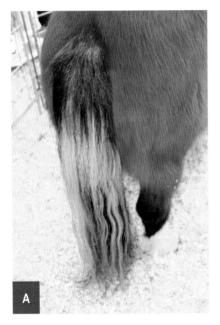

A

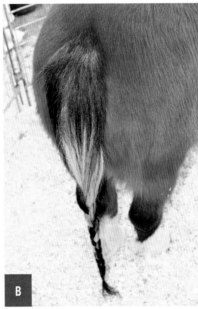

B

6.4 A–D *If you want a long, full tail, protecting it from being stepped on or snagged makes a big difference. Begin with a clean, dry tail (A). Loosely braid the tail and secure it with a braiding elastic (B). Cut from the cuff to the heel of a sock —a tube sock is better if you can find one (C). Tuck the braid into the sock and slip the tie through the loose hair above the braid and below the tailbone. Tie securely (D) . When the top of the tail starts to look ragged or the sock is torn, take the tail down and repeat.*

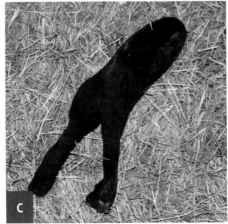

C

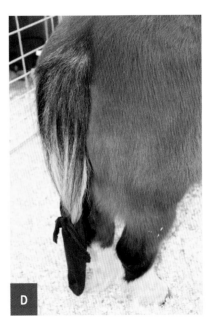

D

your horse's natural defense against insects. To counteract this, you can attach some pieces of string or twine to replace the tail's swishing action, and be very vigilant with a fly sheet and fly spray.

Never braid tight to the tail bone, as this can reduce circulation and cause the tail hair to fall out. There is also a risk when putting a tail up on a horse that is pastured or out with others: he can snag it and instead of pulling out a few hairs, pull out a whole chunk instead because of the braid. Tails that are "put up" need to be taken down and brushed out regularly, whenever the top of the braid starts to look ragged, or (often at my house), whenever the sock is lost or gets a hole in it. Then the long braid will be dragging in the mud and need washing again.

"Less is more! I try to keep clipping to a minimum (bridle path, head, and perhaps fetlocks). Our horses live outside 24/7 so I don't clip unless I'm competing and it's hot out. My favorite gadget is a small air compressor that works wonders to blow dust and dirt out of the coat."

Tamara Chmilar

6.5 *A rubbed-off patch of hair, seen here, especially prior to shedding season, can be a sign of lice.*

Winter Grooming

Other than mane and tail maintenance in the winter, the least amount of grooming is preferable. Especially on cold or wet days, the less you disturb the coat, the better it will be able to do its job. Even the dirt that settles into a thick coat can add insulation and isn't a bad thing.

When there is a nice stretch of weather, however, a thorough grooming to give your horse a proper inspection is a good idea. That thick coat can hide a lot, from poor body condition to skin irritations or external parasites. Traditional grooming tools might not allow you to clean to the skin,

"My Miniature Horses love the dog/cat shedding tool called the FURminator® in the spring for helping to shed out their winter coats."

Tina Silva, Crickhollow Farm

but a blower or vacuum can do a pretty good job. Don't bathe your horse in his winter coat: it is nearly impossible to get him dry to his skin, and you can be setting him up for skin irritation, not to mention catching a chill.

"Creepy Crawlies"

Lice love the thick warm winter coat of a Miniature Horse. And if you have horses, it likely is only a matter of time before you deal with a lice problem in your herd. Luckily, there are treatments that are quite effective (fig. 6.5).

Symptoms of lice include rubbing the hair off, especially on the neck, as well as a rough coat, excessive itching, and even weight loss. Part the hair on the mane and you should be able to see lice, or their eggs, attached to the base of the hair stalk.

If you suspect lice on one horse, then all the horses in contact with him need to be treated, too. Deworming them with an Ivermectin-based dewormer will kill any biting lice, while non-biting lice can be dealt with using dusting powder.

Dusting powder needs to be applied all over every horse, making sure it reaches the skin, and with special attention paid to the topline, where lice like to hang out. This treatment should be repeated after two weeks to get any lice that hatch in that time before they're able to lay eggs and start the cycle all over. When it is spring and warm enough, badly infested horses can be body clipped to make them a less hospitable host.

Some people like to use dusting powder a couple times through the winter months as a preventive measure, rather than waiting for an infestation to happen. Monitoring for lice is important, because it is far better to find and treat than it is to allow your horse to deal with the itching all winter long.

Shedding Season

With as much winter coat as a Miniature Horse has, shedding becomes a very big deal. As soon as the days start getting longer, the hair starts blowing in the wind and is seen on fences, trees, and pastures (fig. 6.6). The more grooming you do during this time, the sooner your horse will turn from the adorable fluffy Thelwell-esque pony you've been enjoying all winter, back into the tiny elegant animal that you know is hiding under there somewhere (fig. 6.7 A & B)!

The transition often won't be pretty, but your horse will appreciate the time you spend grooming because he is so itchy! There are many shedding tools available, from a traditional shedding

6.6 When the days start getting longer, horse hair will start flying!

"A long-toothed dog comb works great for helping shed out winter hair. I like the K9 Competition™ products from Sweden (originally for dogs) for conditioning my Miniature Horses' coats on the outside, as well as rice bran oil taken as a supplement for adding shine from the inside."

Sherry Wilson McEwen, Carousel Miniatures

6.7 A & B A yearling's winter coat is prone to matting as he sheds (A), which can make for a dramatic transformation when you choose to body clip (B).

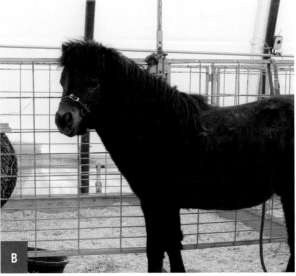

6.8 A & B A variety of grooming tools (here, you see a FURminator® and its results) are available to help remove the shedding winter hair.

blade to all sorts of products to try. One of my favorites is a dog-shedding tool called a FURminator®. It's comfortable to hold, easy to use, and very effective (figs. 6.8 A & B). At the right time though, tools are hardly necessary, and you can pull the hair off with your hands in big clumps.

Yearlings, especially, can be a challenge to get shed out. Their first winter coat is extra thick and is crimped, like sheep's wool, so it mats like sheep's wool. I have done rough clips on yearlings where the coat comes off in one big sheet. Yearlings can shed on their own (better with some elbow grease from you) but many people like to clip them instead, as the transformation is so dramatic and it is fun to see what's underneath that woolly coat. As mentioned, anytime you clip off your horse's coat, it becomes your responsibility to keep him warm, and when you're removing a thick first winter coat, it's going to be quite a difference for the horse. Those yearlings will definitely require a blanket at night and on chilly days for some time.

Sometimes you might find an unpleasant surprise when your horse loses his winter coat—whether lice are discovered during body clipping, or you realize your horse is either much too thin or much too fat underneath all the fur. These issues can be dealt with, but it's much better to be vigilant in your monitoring of your horse's health and body condition through the winter months. Routinely take off your gloves and feel through the hair to check for fat cover, and regularly check for lice.

Chapter 7:
General Health Concerns

Normal Vital Signs

When you go to the Emergency Room, whether you have a stomach flu or a laceration, your vital signs are checked immediately. It is no different with horses, and having an idea of your horse's normal vitals can make it easier to determine when he is in distress, and how worried you need to be.

TPR

The basic vital signs to monitor on horses are their temperature, pulse, and respiration, or TPR. Temperature is taken rectally, and any thermometer will work. Get a digital one from the drug store that beeps when it has recorded a temperature and use a lubricant to make it more comfortable (fig. 7.1).

The horse's pulse (heart rate) can be taken with

NORMAL EQUINE VITAL SIGNS		
	ADULT	**NEWBORN**
TEMPERATURE	99–101°F (37.2–38.3°C)	99.5–102.1°F (37.5–38.9°C)
PULSE	28–44 beats per minute	80–100 beats per minute
RESPIRATION	10–24 breaths per minute	20–40 breaths per minute
MUCOUS MEMBRANES	Moist, healthy pink color	

a stethoscope on his chest behind the left leg, or there is a pulse point inside his jaw. Count beats for 15 seconds, then multiply your number by four to get the number of beats per minute or bpm (fig. 7.2). Use a similar method to calculate your horse's

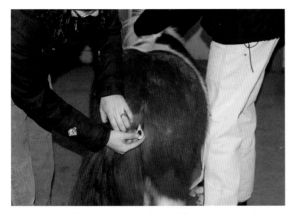

7.1 A digital thermometer works well for monitoring the horse's temperature.

7.2 Using a stethoscope is an easy way to monitor your horse's heart rate.

respiratory rate. Watch his flank rise and fall, or the flaring of his nostrils, for 15 seconds, and then multiply by four to get his breaths per minute.

Monitoring Attitude

BAR and ADR are veterinary acronyms. BAR is good—it stands for Bright, Alert, Responsive, and that's what you want to see from your horse on a regular basis. When he isn't bright, alert, and responsive, this is your warning that something is wrong. Horses, being natural prey animals, work pretty hard at hiding the fact they're not feeling well. Often, the first thing that a conscientious horse owner will notice is that his or her horse simply isn't acting himself—it's hard to put a finger on it, exactly, but the horse just "ain't doin' right." That's what ADR means: Ain't Doin' Right. Anytime you notice your horse is ADR instead of BAR, it's time to get on the phone to your vet.

Routine Veterinary Care

It's important to have a qualified equine veterinarian who you have a good relationship with. Don't wait until you need a vet to find out that the nearest equine practice only does emergencies for existing clients or that the practice is three or more hours away. Research local equine vets as soon (or even before!) you add a Miniature Horse to your family.

Routine veterinary care is the way to both get to know your vet, and to minimize the risk that you'll need him or her on an emergency basis. Horses are, it seems, born to be accident-prone, so chances are you will at some point in your horse ownership life, find yourself standing in a cold barn at two in the morning awaiting the on-call vet. But by keeping up with routine maintenance such as vaccinations, parasite control, and dental care, you'll be doing your due diligence to help keep your horse healthy and happy.

Vaccinations

Routine vaccinations can protect your horse from preventable disease. You can either have your vet administer the vaccinations as part of an annual wellness and dental exam, or you can purchase them and administer them yourself if you are comfortable giving an intramuscular injection and/or administering an intranasal vaccine. The exception is one for rabies, which must be administered by a veterinarian.

Since vaccines are dosed for effectiveness, not weight, a Miniature Horse gets the same amount as a full-sized horse. Follow the directions on the label: most vaccines are 1 ml (milliliter) per dose, but some, such as the Calvenza Flu/Rhino vaccine, are 2 ml, so it's best to check each time you administer it.

Initially, all vaccines need to be boostered at two to four weeks following the first injection to get optimal antibody reaction. Again, check the label on the vaccine you are giving for the optimal timeframe for administration of the booster. Following this initial series, most equine vaccines are given annually to maintain immunity. The exception is for diseases that transfer from horse to horse, such as flu or strangles. In these cases, if your horse is in a high risk situation such as year-round travel or in a busy show barn, a six-month booster might be indicated.

Vaccines for Stay-at-Home Horses

In general, the vaccines that all horses should get regardless of their housing or travel situation are for tetanus, rabies and the mosquito borne diseases,

Eastern and Western sleeping sickness (encephalomyelitis) and West Nile virus. These are diseases not transferred from horse to horse, so even in an isolated herd, or alone, your horse could contract them. All of these diseases are devastating and even if your horse survives, it will involve extensive veterinary care and likely have permanent detriments to your horse's performance and quality of life. While vaccines are not an insignificant cost, especially when you have multiple horses, they become very cheap when you are talking about preventing the loss of your horse.

The other vaccine to consider when you are breeding is the rhino vaccine for pregnant mares. This protects against the abortion strain of rhinopneumonitis (Equine Herpesvirus type 1), and if you have any horses coming and going from your herd, and in contact with your broodmares, it is recommended to vaccinate your mares at five, seven, and nine months gestation.

Vaccines for Horses on the Go
Miniature Horses that go to shows, or travel to clinics or anywhere else where they will encounter other horses, should be additionally vaccinated against communicable diseases. These include influenza, rhinopneumonitis and strangles (*streptococcus equi subsp. equi)*. These are very contagious respiratory diseases that can easily sweep through a barn or show grounds. While life-threatening complications result in a minority of cases, these diseases will make your horse feel awful for a while and the best-case scenario is that you're going to lose your show season while you nurse him back to health. So, when you're investing lots of time and money in getting your horse to perform his very best, make sure you also protect him from the diseases he could encounter along the way.

Ask Your Vet
Before making any decisions on which vaccines are right for your Miniature Horse, it is important to have a discussion with your veterinarian who will be able to make recommendations based on which diseases are most prevalent in your area. Vaccines available vary in their efficacy, and a discussion with your vet allows you to make decisions regarding the level of risk for your individual horse or herd.

With the exception of the strangles and influenza vaccines, which are available as intranasal vaccines, and rabies, which is a separate vaccine that must be administered by a veterinarian, the remainder of the common vaccinations are available in a variety of combinations as a single shot to minimize the number of injections your horse requires. Sometimes these combination shots are more likely to cause a local reaction (swelling at injection site, muscle stiffness, mild fever, lethargy) and your vet will be able to help you make the best decisions.

While it is becoming common with canine vaccines to check titers (and often only vaccinate every three years), reliable titers aren't yet available for most equine vaccines. Therefore, the best option is to follow the vaccine guidelines from the manufacturer and under the guidance of your veterinarian.

Deworming: If You Have Horses, You Have Parasites
Regardless of your diligence in deworming your horses, keeping pastures and paddocks manure free, and generally ensuring the health of your horses, they are still going to have parasites. The goal is to manage the parasite load so that it never gets to the point where it impacts their health.

Modern Parasite Control

In the past, it was recommended you deworm on a regular schedule—usually every two to six months, depending on the management situation—and rotate the products used in the hopes that any parasite in your horses' system would be susceptible to one of the products used. Today, we have a growing issue with resistance to the drugs available to deworm horses, and routine deworming is no longer recommended. Instead, by only deworming those horses that need it, we are both reducing the opportunity for the parasites to develop resistance to the products available, and also avoiding unnecessary medication of our horses.

Fecal Egg Counts and Targeted Deworming

Current research supports routine fecal egg counts (FEC). Simply collect a manure sample from your

Vaccinating Your Miniature Horse

When you have some experience, you can often purchase your own vaccinations and administer them. Most vaccines are given intramuscularly, which means they are injected into the large muscles of the body.

These vaccines are sold in single doses with a needle included. Often this is a 1 ½-inch, 18-gauge needle provided with a 1000-pound horse in mind; for your Miniature Horse that is only a quarter of the size, you don't need a needle that big, and it will make the whole process go a lot smoother if you switch that needle out for a 1-inch, 20-gauge needle instead.

Injections should be given in the large muscle masses: the neck, the hindquarters, or pectoral. The neck is often the easiest and safest. You want to inject right into the middle of the large muscle of the neck: trace a triangle shape between the nuchal ligament that runs just below the crest, the line of the shoulder, and the vertebrae of the neck above the jugular furrow, and choose a point at the center (fig. 7.3).

Taking a pinch or tent of skin near your chosen injection site can help distract your horse from the poke. Insert the needle in one smooth motion, right to the hilt. Be sure to draw back on the syringe before injecting to ensure that you are not in a vein: when there is blood in the syringe

7.3 An intramuscular injection, which is how many vaccines are given, can be administered in the triangle formed by the shoulder, the nuchal ligament that runs just below the horse's neck, and the vertebrae of the neck.

horse—a few balls will do—package it in a sealed baggie with his name on it, and keep it cool until you are able to deliver it to your vet, within 24 hours. Check with the clinic before you collect the sample to make sure it's a day they're accepting FEC samples.

The test will determine how many parasite eggs are being shed in your horse's manure, and, therefore, how heavy the parasite load is (fig. 7.4).

Based on this information, your horse will be classified as a *high shedder, moderate shedder*, or *low shedder*.

In any herd of horses, there are likely a few high shedders that require more frequent deworming to keep their parasite load in check and prevent them from shedding eggs to infest their pasturemates. Many horses will be low shedders, and not require as frequent deworming. Following routine

or showing at the hub of the needle, withdraw and start all over—you must not inject the vaccine into a vein. When you are sure you are in the right spot, depress the plunger to give the vaccine. Withdraw and rub the area where the needle was seated. There may be a little bleeding following the injection. Watch closely for any reaction. Serious vaccine reactions take place almost immediately following injection and are very rare. More common vaccine reactions happen over the next day and include muscle soreness, swelling, and general malaise. When you have any concerns, speak to your vet immediately.

If you choose to give the vaccine in the hindquarters, first be aware of kicking. Do not give the injection up high on the horse's hip because if there were a localized reaction, it wouldn't be able to drain. Instead, inject into the hamstring muscle below the point of the buttock. Stand off to the side, with the horse's hip against yours to keep yourself in a safe position, and consider detaching the needle from the syringe, then re-attaching once the needle is seated with no blood showing at the hub.

If you have an interest in doing some of your own intramuscular vaccinations, ask your veterinarian give you a tutorial.

The strangles vaccine is given intranasally, which means it is sprayed up the nostril. The vaccine is a modified live version, which means that it carries live bacteria. For this reason, you need to be very careful not to contaminate any needles and inadvertently inject the strangles vaccine. Although it is not possible for the horse to contract the strangles disease from the vaccine due to the modifications made to the bacteria, it will cause a nasty abscess. For best practices, do all your injectable vaccines on a separate day before you administer the strangles vaccine.

This vaccine comes in two vials, and you need to draw up the liquid and mix it into the powder to reconstitute it. Then draw it up into the syringe, replace the needle with the applicator provided, and administer it up your horse's nostril. He won't like it, so be quick. Only a small amount of the product needs to get onto the mucous membrane for it be effective, so don't worry if he immediately snorts what appears to be all of it back out again.

fecal egg counts in your herd, your vet can help you determine which horses require more frequent deworming, and which do not.

Any of your high shedders should be rechecked two weeks following deworming, which is referred to as a fecal egg count reduction test (FECRT). This checks that the deworming product you used was effective. When the FECRT shows any remaining parasite load, there is resistance to the deworming product, and deworming should be repeated with a different product and the FECRT checked again to ensure you are effectively ridding your horse of the parasites.

Even when using targeted deworming, all horses should be dewormed annually. Since FECs don't effectively detect all types of parasites, an annual deworming ensures you are staying on top of things. When you are based in a place with a cold winter climate, waiting until after a killing frost is the ideal time for the annual deworming because your horses won't immediately be infested again (fig. 7.5).

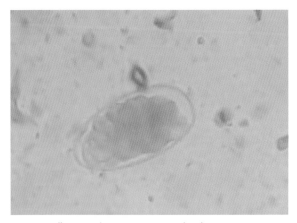

7.4 A small strongyle parasite egg under the microscope during a fecal egg count.

An Ounce of Prevention

Parasite control is important. Neglecting it can result in serious health concerns, from general poor condition and performance issues, all the way up to colic and death. If you have a horse you feel may have a high parasite load, deworm only under the recommendation and supervision of your veterinarian. A sudden kill of a large parasite load can cause a serious, potentially deadly, impaction colic.

It is much safer—and cheaper—to follow the recommended guidelines for parasite control and invest in FECs and deworming medication, rather than a colic treatment or the loss of your horse.

Young Horses

Young horses are susceptible to different parasites than adult horses, and, therefore, need to follow a different protocol. The most common parasite to afflict weanlings and yearlings is the ascarid, which is commonly called a roundworm. Ascarids are the largest parasite, and can reach up to three feet in length in just three months. You can imagine that could cause serious issues in the digestive tract of a yearling Miniature Horse.

7.5 Deworming your horse involves squirting paste or liquid into his mouth.

7.6 *Removal of manure from your horse's environment is an important part of parasite control.*

To prevent ascarids from reaching their full size and becoming dangerous, it is important to deworm young horses every two months, with a product that is appropriate for roundworms. Foals should be dewormed starting at two months of age then every two months thereafter until they are a year old, when they can begin on the adult protocol of FECs and targeted deworming.

Dewormers are dosed by weight, and sometimes it can be a challenge to measure a dose of paste dewormer, especially for a two-month-old Miniature foal. It can be helpful to draw the paste out of the tube into a smaller syringe for accurate measurement, and to avoid an accident when the locking mechanism on the measurement scale on the tube provided fails to function properly. Any overdose should be immediately reported to your veterinarian who can tell you which symptoms to watch for and determine if your horse needs any treatment.

Luckily, most dewormers are quite safe. The exception is moxidectin that is sold under the brand name Quest®. This product is dosed assuming a certain percentage of muscle in the body weight, and it can be easy to have an overdose even when you feel it has been dosed accurately in Miniature Horses, as well as ponies, donkeys, and young horses. As there are other products available, it is best to completely avoid moxidectin unless you have an accurate weight for your horse and a medical reason for using it (for example, if your horse has shown resistance to the other dewormers).

Scoop That Poop

One of the best things you can do to minimize your horse's exposure to parasites is to pick up manure from his environment (fig. 7.6). In addition, anytime you add a new horse to your herd, keep him isolated, carefully pick up all the manure, and be vigilant about ensuring your existing horses don't have access to the new horse until after you have been able to do a FEC, dewormed as necessary, then done a FECRT two weeks after deworming to check the efficacy of your deworming product. Only then is it safe to allow the horse in with your herd.

Different herds have different parasites, and different strains of parasites, and you don't want to inadvertently introduce a particularly resistant strain into your herd's environment that you will then have to battle in the future. The warmer the climate, the more virulent the parasites are because they are able to maintain their lifecycle without the interruption of the inhospitable environment of winter. When you bring in a horse from a more temperate climate, or one from a more intensive management system, it is even more important to quarantine him from your herd until after you have dealt with any parasite load he may have.

Alternative Deworming Products

There is recent interest in the use of "natural" dewormers, such as diatomaceous earth, garlic, and other mixtures of herbs. There is not currently any evidence that these products, or any other non-commercial dewormers, are effective in removing parasites from your horse's system. If you do choose to use an alternative to chemical deworming, please do so only after checking with your vet, and follow up with a fecal egg count to confirm the effectiveness of the product you used. Some feed additives, garlic included, can be toxic in the right amounts and you don't want to do harm to your horse while intending to help him.

Dental Care

Proper maintenance of your Miniature Horse's teeth is vital to health, performance, and longevity. But before we get into that, here is a little bit about how your horse's teeth work in the first place.

Like baby humans, foals are generally born without teeth. Their baby teeth come in starting at two weeks of age. These baby teeth, or "caps," are then shed as the horse ages, and by the time they are five years old, they should have a full set of adult teeth.

Horses' adult teeth, unlike a human's, continue to erupt throughout their lives. As they chew their food, the tooth is gradually worn away, and more and more of the tooth erupts from the tooth socket to replace it. As they age, their incisors often appear longer, especially the incisors that aren't as involved in the grinding of food—hence the term, "long in the tooth." Because of this process, it is possible for a knowledgeable person to find the approximate age of the horse by assessing the degree of eruption and wear of the teeth. This gives us another colloquialism, "Don't look a gift horse in the mouth."

Floating

The horse's upper jaw is a tiny bit wider than the lower jaw, which means that as the teeth wear, the outside edge of the upper teeth and the inside edge of the lower teeth aren't ground down at the same rate as the rest of the teeth. These edges can become very sharp, cutting the tongue and inner cheeks. Some horses also develop hooks at the front or the back of their cheek teeth (premolars and molars) because they're not perfectly aligned.

These irregularities can cause the horse a great deal of discomfort, resulting in weight loss and bitting issues. Other problems can arise as the result of uneven wear. For example, should the horse lose a tooth, the opposing tooth will have nothing to grind against, but will continue to erupt at the same rate, resulting in a "step" that will bind and interfere with chewing.

Routine dental care involves "floating" or leveling out the teeth to eliminate the sharp points and hooks that interfere with the grinding action. Floating involves files or a "power float," which is an electric grinding wheel. Some horses need to be floated rarely, while others require frequent floating, especially if they have an ongoing issue being addressed. Horses only have about 3 millimeters of crown protecting the pulp cavity of their teeth, so any teeth that need extensive reduction must be done gradually, allowing time between floats to allow the pulp cavity to recede. Should the pulp cavity be reached, not only will it be very painful for the horse because it opens up an avenue for infection, but it can result in the death of the tooth, causing more issues in the long run. Additionally, horses only have a finite amount of tooth to last them their whole lives; unnecessarily aggressive reductions will decrease the life of the tooth and, potentially, the life of the horse.

Vet or Dentist?

So who do you trust with such an important portion of your horse's health and welfare? Unlike with humans, where dentists are highly trained and overseen by a governing body to ensure they have the knowledge and skill to care for your teeth, there is no such standardized training or certification for equine dentists at this time. While you might get a good one, when you don't— and the dentist does irreparable damage to your

7.7 A veterinarian has the equipment, knowledge, and resources to maintain your horse's teeth for peak health and performance. Dr. Crystal Lee of Burwash Equine floats Circle J Dezigner Genes to ensure he is comfortable with the bit prior to show season.

horse's mouth—there is absolutely no recourse. And word of mouth is not a reliable form of recommendation, as most people don't have the knowledge to know if what was done to their horse was appropriate.

I choose not to allow anyone but a qualified equine veterinarian to provide dental care (fig. 7.7). Among all the treatment considerations we've discussed, it isn't possible to properly evaluate and treat potential hooks at the back of the mouth without sedation. It is illegal for anyone but

Miniature Tales
Sonic and Cruise

Sonic was my grandad's horse and had been driven as part of his hitch, including in the Calgary Stampede parade. After a couple years off, Sonic came to me and I was keen to get him driving single, as I'd long admired his movement. While ground-driving him to bring him back into training, I found he was very uncomfortable with the bit, constantly mouthing, holding his mouth open, and twisting his upper lip in discomfort. I confirmed with Grandad that this was unusual for him, and then switched to working him without a bit until I could have the vet out to do his teeth.

Sure enough the vet found a very large, razor sharp hook at the front of his lower cheek teeth on each side (fig. 7.8). With the issue properly addressed and the hooks reduced, Sonic once again was completely comfortable with a bit in his mouth and returned to training with great enthusiasm.

Unfortunately, it is far too easy to get wrapped up in your goals for a horse and see such a reaction as misbehavior. Imagine if I had followed the

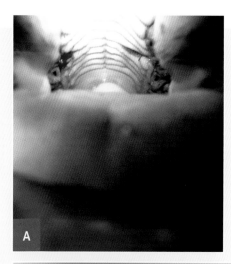

A

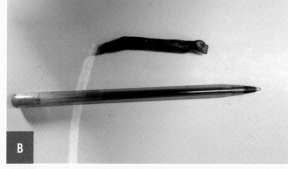

B

7.9 A & B This stick, which had been stuck in his mouth, must have been very painful for Cruise, but he gave no external signs that anything was wrong.

common advice to tighten his noseband or put a flash noseband on him? What sort of pain and damage could I have caused?

On the other side of the coin, Miniature Horses can be extremely stoic. Dr. Crystal Lee was preparing to do a routine float on her own Miniature Horse, Excels High C Cruise, when she was surprised to discover a stick wedged sideways in the roof of his mouth. Despite no external symptoms or change in behavior—Cruise even behaved normally with a bit in his mouth—the stick had to have been quite painful, wearing large sores at each end (figs. 7.9 A & B).

These two stories demonstrate why routine dental exams by your veterinarian are an important part of keeping your horse healthy and comfortable.

7.8 A razor sharp point like this one—and the matching one on the other side—was the very good reason for Sonic's discomfort with the bit.

a qualified veterinarian to administer IV sedation to your horse. Even if it wasn't against the law, IV sedation is a risk, and a veterinarian is trained not only to safely dose and administer the drugs, but to deal with any side effects and reactions. Veterinarians are highly educated in dental care and are carefully monitored and held to a high standard of care.

This decision is a personal one, but armed with a little more knowledge about what is involved you'll be able to make the right choice for your horse's health and well-being.

Performance Issues

When you have a performance horse you are preparing for any sort of competition, your relationship with your local equine veterinary practice becomes even more important. When you notice anything out of the ordinary in your Miniature Horse's performance, looking into it sooner rather than later can save the horse's career. Remember, horses only have so many ways of telling you that something is wrong, so always investigate every possible avenue and source of pain as a potential cause of misbehavior.

Complementary Treatment Modalities

Working together with your veterinarian, trained equine body workers can help your horse be as comfortable as possible as you work toward his athletic potential. Working with a massage therapist or other bodywork

professional helps contribute to your horse's long-term soundness or can be used to treat a specific issue. They'll also be able to work with you to help create a routine of stretches or other exercises individualized for your horse (fig. 7.10).

Lameness Exams

Lameness can sometimes be very subtle, and might not become evident without a thorough veterinary lameness exam. Flexion tests, nerve blocks, and other diagnostics help your vet pinpoint the area where your horse is experiencing pain, and diagnostic imaging with ultrasound, radiographs, or even MRI can help diagnose the issue and make a plan to help him return to performance soundness. When you notice a performance issue or misbehavior, lameness could very well be the cause.

The Lameness Locator® is new technology available to veterinarians that uses inertial sensors to track your horse's strides and determine the

7.10 Circle J On The Rocks very much enjoys his body-work from Teresa Valois Humpage of Freedom in Motion Equine Therapy. Teresa has been an integral part of Rocky's athletic development.

source of the lameness. It allows even the most subtle lameness to be much more easily identified. In addition to being a great tool to assist in diagnosis, the Lameness Locator also enables your vet to quantify the response to nerve blocks or treatment, so the percentage of improvement is no longer subjective. This cutting-edge tool works just as effectively on Miniature Horses as it does on horses of full size.

Gastroscopy

The most recent studies suggest that 17 to 58 percent of show and sport horses suffer from gastric ulcers at some point in their career, which definitely impacts their performance. As mentioned before, Miniature Horses are no exception, and the diverse symptoms that can be shown by horses with ulcers can make it more difficult to realize your horse needs assistance. Horses with gastric ulcers may not be doing well (underweight, poor hair coat), prefer to eat their hay instead of their grain or concentrate, lie down while eating, have repetitive minor episodes of colic, or show behavioral issues during performance.

A gastroscope is the only concrete method of diagnosing gastric ulcers. A camera is passed into the horse's stomach so the vet can visually inspect the lining of the stomach for lesions. However, given that Miniature Horses need a much smaller dosage of Gastrogard® and it is a very effective treatment, sometimes veterinarians will prescribe a trial of Gastrogard to see if it resolves the symptoms, and use the response to treatment to make their diagnosis.

Without proper treatment, ulcers do not heal on their own. Even following a full course of daily treatment with the appropriate medication prescribed by your veterinarian to heal the lesion, steps must be taken to prevent the recurrence. Continued use of the medication during times of stress may be recommended, but most important will be management changes: increased feeding of roughage, use of slow-feed hay nets, and increasing turnout time are among the changes your vet may recommend. After a full course of treatment with Gastrogard, it may also be recommended to recheck the gastroscopy to ensure that the ulcers have resolved and no further treatment is required.

In 35 years of owning, breeding, and showing Miniature Horses, we've never had a horse that required treatment for gastric ulcers. Lucky? Yeah, definitely. But I suspect that our outdoor management of all our horses, including performance horses, as well as a strongly forage-based diet, has a lot to do with our good luck.

Building a Relationship

Demonstrating loyalty to any business has its perks. Whether it's a tire shop, a plumber, or a restaurant, being a frequent good customer who pays her bills on time benefits you in the long run, with loyalty discounts and an overall improved experience. When you're talking about the health and well-being of your horses, this is even more important. Developing a long-term relationship with your equine veterinary practice also means that your vet will always have easy access to your horse's complete medical history and is invested in his health and success.

The veterinary community is a small one. If you are bouncing from clinic to clinic and leaving unpaid balances at all of them, you are burning bridges that your horse's life might depend

Miniature Tales
Ivan's Chief

Ivan's Chief was purchased by my friend Christine at an "Odd & Unusual" auction sale. A tiny, fuzzy yearling, it wasn't until Christine got him home that she realized what bad shape he was in. Skinny, wormy, and lousy, Chief needed a lot of TLC before he began to thrive.

Christine had to do some research to track down his registration paperwork, and in the process discovered the Chief had traveled, already in his short life, all the way from the eastern United States to the other side of the continent on Vancouver Island then back east again to Innisfail, Alberta, before he found his way to Airdrie and into Christine's life.

Several years later, Chief was a mature stallion, and doing very well in the show ring at local AMHA shows (figs. 7.11 A & B). With Championships in halter and country pleasure driving, Christine decided to travel a bit farther from home and took Chief to a show in Saskatchewan, about a nine-hour drive from home.

Chief just wasn't himself on the trip. He didn't eat well, was dull and lethargic, and Christine ended up scratching him from his classes as he clearly wasn't right. Back home, Christine immediately consulted her veterinarian and they discussed the possibility of ulcers, starting him on a daily dose of Gastrogard. Immediately, he showed improvement, and through the rest of his show career his gastric health was carefully monitored and

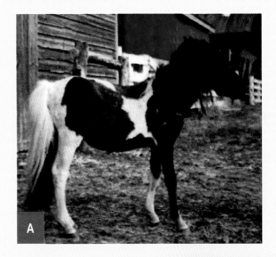

7.11 A & B Ivan's Chief soon after he was purchased at auction (A) and as an adult stallion (B).

treated, especially any time that a long haul was involved.

Given his early history, the longer-than-usual trip was even more stressful than for an average horse. Stress of any kind can cause gastric ulcers, and any time performance or behavior is impacted, a call to your vet is warranted.

on one day. Be a good client; pay your bill on time, work out a payment plan for those times you can't, follow instructions for your horse's care, and be pleasant.

Emergencies

Not all clinics offer 24-hour emergency care. If your clinic doesn't, make sure you know who they recommend. Get the emergency number, put it in your phone, post it in your barn, your horse trailer, and anywhere else you might need it.

When you're not sure if you have a real emergency, call anyway. Your veterinarian would much rather talk to you for a few minutes and determine that it can wait until Monday, than not be called until it is too late to do anything.

Colic

Colic is the general term for any sort of abdominal discomfort in horses. Colic is the number one killer of horses, so anytime you see the symptoms in your horse, you need to consider it an emergency and get on the phone to your vet. While waiting for your vet to arrive, it is best to remove all feed. Most of the time the colic will resolve with treatment, but for the times that it is more serious, early diagnosis and intervention from your vet can make a huge difference in your horse's chances for survival, especially if he is a surgical candidate.

Lacerations

Any sort of wound that is full thickness through the skin should be examined by your veterinarian, and the sooner the better. Wounds can only be successfully sutured within a few hours of happening, so time is of the essence to give them the best chance to heal. Any wound that is near a joint (even a seemingly minor wound) has the potential to cause serious harm by introducing infection to the joint itself. These wounds should be examined by a vet to determine whether the joint might be involved. Additionally, any time a wound is causing lameness, it is best to have the horse examined.

Horses are good at getting injured, even when you think you've done everything you can to keep them safe with appropriate fencing and good management practices. The good news is that they are usually equally good at healing. With proper treatment from your vet and diligent care from you, the most gruesome wounds can heal very well.

Not Eating

As a grazing animal, food is the first priority of any horse. If your Miniature Horse turns his nose up at his dinner, it's time to be concerned. Lack of

Symptoms of Colic

- Not eating, especially right at feeding time
- Acting depressed, dull, or disinterested
- Frequent lying down and standing up again
- Curling upper lip or yawning
- Looking at or biting at sides
- Pawing
- Rolling or thrashing (severely colicky horses can injure themselves or those around them)
- Refusal to stand
- Lack of gut sounds
- Lack of manure production
- Posturing to urinate without urinating
- Elevated pulse

appetite is a concerning symptom in any horse, but in Miniature Horses, inappetence can trigger hyperlipemia, a condition where the fat stores are dumped into the bloodstream, overwhelming internal organs and often leading to organ failure and death. If your horse gets hyperlipemic, it won't matter what problem caused him to lose his appetite in the first place because he'll be in a serious, life-threatening condition very quickly.

Be proactive. Any time your Miniature Horse refuses to eat, make that call to your vet.

Lameness

There are many causes of sudden lameness, some serious, some not so much, but all painful for your horse. If your horse is limping, he is in pain, and you should consult your vet. It could be an active process like laminitis (see more about this on p. 83), which needs to be controlled as soon as possible to minimize long-term damage. It could be a sole abscess, which is extremely painful but usually straightforward for your veterinarian to treat and get your horse quickly on the road to recovery. Or, it could be any number of other things, all of which benefit from veterinary care. Don't leave your Miniature Horse limping around (fig. 7.12).

Eye Injury

Many people don't realize that a swollen, weepy eye is an emergency, but with any sort of eye injury, time is of the essence. Eye trauma, most commonly a corneal ulcer, needs appropriate medication as soon and as often as possible to give the eye the best chance at healing. More serious issues require even more intensive treatment, and possibly hospitalization or consultation with an ophthalmologist.

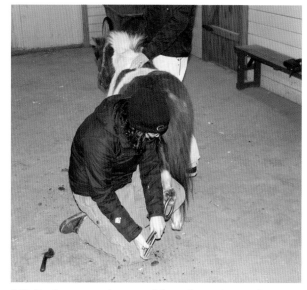

7.12 Hoof testers are just one of the tools veterinarians have at their disposal to help diagnose the source of your horse's lameness.

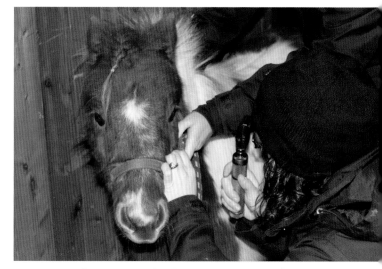

7.13 Dr. Crystal Lee uses an ophthalmoscope to look inside the eye and identify any abnormalities.

Since horses rely heavily on their vision to feel safe, they won't hold an eye closed or squinted unless it is very painful. Any time your horse is reluctant to hold his eye wide open, he is very uncomfortable and requires treatment (fig. 7.13).

Choke

"Choke" in horses refers to the condition of getting feed material stuck in their esophagus. It doesn't close off their airway (trachea) like it does in humans, but it is still very distressing for them, and if not promptly treated, can lead to aspiration pneumonia, colic, and other issues. You'll see them coughing, pawing, and looking in distress, often with saliva and food in their nostrils. Choke cases virtually always require veterinary intervention and the sooner the better.

Diarrhea

Diarrhea in horses can be a symptom of some of the more infectious diseases, and some of them are so contagious that only a veterinary clinic with proper isolation facilities will even admit them. Even if not associated with an infectious disease, diarrhea itself can cause a horse to become dangerously dehydrated very quickly—in foals especially. Horses with diarrhea often require intensive treatment on IV fluids to recover.

Hoof Care

Why It Matters

As with any horse, Miniature Horses require routine hoof care to keep them sound, healthy, and pain free. Just as your fingernails continue to grow and have to be trimmed regularly, so will a horse's feet. And if you've ever had to spend a day on your feet in ill-fitting shoes, you know how a horse feels when his feet aren't properly trimmed.

Frequency

Six to eight weeks is a good guideline for routine trims, but pay attention to your horse and see when he needs hoof care (figs. 7.14 A–E). Foals tend to require more frequent trimming, as well as horses that have previous issues with laminitis or that have an imbalance that must be corrected.

As previously mentioned, routine care between trims is important as well. Regularly cleaning out your horse's feet helps prevent infections such as thrush, a bacterial and/or fungal infection of the sulci (the deep grooves alongside the frog), as well as removing rocks that could

---

Suggested First Aid Kit

(Courtesy of Burwash Equine Services)

- Phone number of veterinarian
- List of normal temperature, pulse, and respiration
- Bandage scissors
- Thermometer
- Stethoscope
- Flashlight
- Hoof pick
- Clean bucket
- Lip twitch
- Electrolytes
- Hand sanitizer
- Latex gloves
- Antiseptic scrub and solutions (Betadine® or Hibitane®)
- Antibiotic ointment (Hibitane, Silvadene®, or Derma Gel®)
- Antibiotic Wound Spray (Vetericyn®)

- 4 x 4 gauze sponges
- Non-adhesive dressing (Telfa™)
- Roll gauze
- Gamgee, sheet cotton, or quilted stable wrap
- Vetrap®
- Lightplast®
- Duct tape
- Paper towels
- Disposable diapers (for foot bandages)
- Syringes (12cc, 60cc)
- Bute or Banamine®
- PVC pipe for splints

The "Golden Rule" of first aid kits: The contents are for emergency use only! And when used, they should be immediately replaced.

7.14 A–E *An experienced farrier is able to expertly take care of your horse's hoof maintenance and any other issues with the feet. Here, farrier Hans Kollewyn trims North Star's Valdez Y Basan.*

cause a bruised sole—and just generally getting your horse more comfortable with having his feet handled (fig. 7.15). When picking up your horse's feet is just part of the usual handling routine, your farrier visits will go much more smoothly.

There are lots of farriers who won't trim Miniature Horses, and it is in a large part due to the fact that too many people don't expect the same standards of behavior from their horses as they would a full-sized horse. Teach your Miniature Horse to be relaxed and comfortable with having his feet picked up on a regular basis and you'll go a long way to making him a good equine citizen and removing the stigma that Miniature Horses are bad about their feet.

Farrier or DIY?

It is common for people to do their own trimming, but just be sure you have the knowledge before tackling this responsibility. Improper trims can cause all sorts of issues, and there can be long-lasting repercussions for your horse from a mistake.

An experienced farrier will have the training and skill not only to maintain your horse's feet, but to correct any issues that may arise. In young horses, proper trimming can improve minor limb crookedness, and a good farrier can mean the difference between pain and future soundness for laminitic horses.

Farriers can be expensive, especially when you have a number of horses, but as with most things in life, you get what you pay for. Sometimes a good happy medium is to learn basic trimming so you can maintain those horses with no concerns for most of the year then have your qualified farrier do any young or special-needs horses and trim everyone once or twice a year to make sure that you are keeping everything on track, balanced, and healthy.

7.15 Routine cleaning of your horse's feet can help prevent and recognize any issues that may come up, as well as accustom your horse to calmly accept handling of his feet.

Chapter 8:

Serious Health Concerns for Miniature Horses

Major Problems Commonly Seen

While all horses are susceptible to the same health risks, there are a few serious medical issues that are more commonly seen in Miniature Horses.

Laminitis

Laminitis, or as it is often known, "founder," is a painful inflammation of the tissues (laminae) that bond the coffin bone to the inside of the hoof wall. A potentially crippling lameness, laminitis is often associated with overweight Miniature Horses, but there are other causes as well (fig. 8.1).

8.1 The distinctive shape of the feet of a horse with chronic laminitic changes.

Symptoms

In the acute phase of laminitis, horses experience severe pain in both front feet, or occasionally, all four. They prefer to stand in a "rocked-back" posture in an attempt to take weight off their front feet, and when asked to move, do so very reluctantly, with a "walking-on-eggshells" gait. They have increased pulses to the affected feet and spend more time lying down.

What's Happening?

Inflammatory mediators are produced that cause damage to the sensitive laminae inside the hoof capsule. As these tiny structures are damaged, they are no longer able to perform their function of holding the coffin bone in place. The coffin bone starts to rotate, and the tip of the bone then applies pressure on the sole of the foot. In extreme cases, the coffin bone actually works its way through the sole of the hoof, an extremely painful condition that often necessitates euthanasia to end a horse's suffering.

Miniature Tales
Founder February

One year, in February, several of our geldings foundered. They were out on winter pasture, a stubble field, and should not have had access to any feed that would have caused their issues. To this day we don't have any idea what caused it, but they were treated with anti-inflammatories and careful management of their feet moving forward. Two of them recovered very quickly, but the other two were more severely affected.

After several years of careful hoof care and management of feed, Finnegan, at the age of 15, was able to return to full soundness and was back in the show ring winning Roadster championships as he had been in his younger days. Jerome, on the other hand, is managing well and is comfortable, but we are skeptical that he will ever return to performance soundness. As a result, he is moving on to a new career, one that will be low impact, working as part of a therapy program.

Today we continue to carefully manage the other two horses, as well, watching their intake of green grass and monitoring their body condition, as well as careful maintenance of their hoof care, even though they haven't had any further issues.

Laminitis is a serious problem and one that you may have to face even with careful management. However, with proper follow-up care, and depending on the severity, it doesn't have to be the end of a performance career or a life.

Causes

While being overweight and the accompanying insulin resistance is the biggest risk factor for laminitis, there are many other causes: spring grass, overload of grain, or any sudden intake high in sugars can cause a horse to develop it. Horses with metabolic disorders (also common in Miniature Horses) have an increased risk and must be managed carefully to mitigate the dangers of feed-related triggers. PPID (Equine Cushing's Disease) may also predispose horses to laminitis and should be treated as necessary to manage this risk.

Any major stressor can cause a horse to develop laminitis. Surgery, trauma, and infections, such as a retained placenta in a broodmare or pneumonia, all have the risk of laminitis as a complication. "Mechanical founder" is also a possibility with the concussion of working on a hard surface or if a supporting limb bears excess weight following an injury to the opposing leg.

Prevention

Keeping your Miniature Horse at a healthy weight and monitoring his intake of high risk feeds is the best chance to prevent laminitis. When your horse shows any lameness, immediate veterinary intervention will help minimize the damage and give your horse the best chance at returning to full soundness in the future.

Treatment

Acute flare-ups of laminitis are treated with anti-inflammatories, icing of the affected feet, and padding with boots, and/or keeping the horse on deep bedding to help him be more comfortable, as well as modification of his diet to help stop the inflammatory process. As he becomes more comfortable, radiographs of the feet will determine if they have any coffin bone rotation, and determining the degree of the rotation will help your farrier with trimming decisions. Consistent, careful trimming by a knowledgeable farrier will be crucial to your horse's chances of returning to soundness.

Once he has had one episode of laminitis, your horse will be very prone to another flare-up. The more episodes he has, the greater the damage and the greater the likelihood that he will never return to full soundness. Careful management on your part, and working closely with your vet and farrier, will give your horse the best chance.

Metabolic Disorders

Miniature Horses, as with other "easy-keeping" breeds of horses, are prone to metabolic issues. These hormone imbalances are most often seen in middle-aged and elderly horses, and can make them prone to many other health issues.

Current thought would combine these under the heading of *Equine Metabolic Syndrome*. Characterized by hormone imbalance, horses with EMS are the stereotypical easy-keepers that seem to develop fat deposits "on air." Abnormal fat deposits form specifically over the crest of the neck, the back, and the tail head. These horses are insulin resistant, so show high levels of insulin in the face of normal levels of glucose when tested. This syndrome may go hand in hand with PPID or may precede the development of PPID.

Pituitary Pars Intermedia Dysfunction (PPID), more commonly called Equine Cushing's Disease, is a dysfunction of the pituitary gland. Most common in older horses (15 years and older), PPID causes increased production of cortisol, a stress hormone, and ACTH (adrenocorticotropic hormone). This hormone imbalance causes all sorts of health issues in the elderly horse, from laminitis and muscle wasting, immune suppression (and, therefore, heightened susceptibility to disease) and poor energy, to weight loss and a long, curly, non-shedding coat. Horses tested positive for PPID can be treated with a daily medication prescribed by your veterinarian that is very effective in improving the hormone imbalance and decreasing the clinical signs, but they must remain on the medication for the rest of their lives or the symptoms will return.

While these disorders have differing causes, the early warning signs are the same. Horses with abnormal fat deposits in their crest, tail head, and over their eyes, and horses that are generally overweight are at an increased risk.

Prevention

While some horses are simply predisposed to metabolic disorders, you can limit the risk of developing laminitis as well by carefully managing their feed. Green grass, particularly in the spring or after a frost is particularly dangerous. Any feed high in carbohydrates is converted in the digestive system to sugar and increases the risk. There are commercial feeds developed specifically for horses with metabolic issues, with low starch and carbohydrates, and hay rations can be soaked and then removed from the water prior to feeding to further reduce the sugar content.

Diagnosis

Your veterinarian can do a blood panel to test for all three different metabolic disorders, and routine monitoring of bloodwork for older horses can be beneficial. Once diagnosis is confirmed, your veterinarian can make a recommendation regarding management and potential medication.

Management

Feeding your metabolic horse will be the biggest part of their management, though exercise and activity is also beneficial in controlling his weight. Your vet can help you make a plan that is specific to your horse and situation, and depending on your horse's bloodwork and diagnosis, the plan may include daily medication.

Any senior horse is at risk for developing PPID. If an elderly horse shows any symptoms that may be indicative of a metabolic issue, or even as a routine screening, a metabolic blood panel gives you the information to treat him and help prevent the potential for laminitis.

Miniature Tales

Robin

Circle J Robin was a 23-year-old retired broodmare, and I'd spent all winter with her in the barn at night, pouring senior feed into her to try to keep her at a healthy weight, despite her annual fall dental work. In the springtime, with the advent of the green grass, she finally started to pick up. One morning in June, I looked at her as I was turning her out and thought that she was finally at a healthy weight, with her ribs covered. The next morning, she was lame on all four legs, reluctant to walk, and down more than she wanted to stand. After a couple days in a deeply bedded stall and on Banamine® for inflammation and pain relief, she recovered quickly, and I kept her off grass. I had Cushings in the back of my mind, even though she had no other symptoms: no fat deposits, she shed her coat well, and generally didn't "look" like a Cushing's horse.

The following winter, in the middle of February, with absolutely no change in feed or management, Robin foundered again. We had the vet out right away to pull blood, and sure enough, the results came back that she was positive for all three metabolic disorders. Within a week of starting her on Cushing's medication, Robin no longer needed the Banamine and was getting around well. Three months later we rechecked her bloodwork and it showed the Cushing's was well controlled. Robin is still kept off grass and on a low sugar diet to be safe, but she is doing very well on her daily medication.

Shortly after Robin was diagnosed, her 25-year-old companion, Image, looked a bit off for a few days. He wasn't nearly as painful as Robin, but again, had no change in feed or management (and was already on a low-sugar diet because he was 25 years old and lived with Robin). When it was time for Robin's bloodwork to be rechecked, we had Image tested as well. He was also positive for PPID.

Since Image wasn't actively laminitic when we started him on the medication, I didn't anticipate seeing a change in him. I was wrong—I hadn't realized how subdued he had become until he was on medication and started feeling better. Suddenly, he was his old, boisterous, playful self, racing around (carefully, as Image is also blind), bucking and showing off for his special girlfriend, Robin.

Both horses are on a careful routine of hoof care to maintain their feet (as they now have a history of laminitis), as well as their daily medication, and are now 25 and 26 years of age and doing very well.

Upward Fixation of the Patella

Horses have a unique apparatus in their stifle that allows them to lock their hind legs in place, so that they can doze while standing up. This is an evolved safety feature for a flight animal, allowing them to be on their feet and ready to run away from danger while still catching some rest. A ligament slides over a groove in their stifle joint and holds the limb in place. It's a pretty neat tool, but the problem arises when the ligament stays in a locked position, holding the patella in the upward position and the joint stuck in place when a horse tries to move off.

When the stifle locks in place it can look quite alarming. The hind leg is straight and the horse sort of drags it along behind him. It is easy to think it is broken or something else seriously wrong, but generally it unlocks on its own after a few steps.

Predisposing Factors

Horses with a straight-leg conformation are more likely to develop upward fixation of the patella than those with normal hind-limb angulation. A focus on correct conformation in your breeding program will help minimize the risk.

It is interesting to note that upward fixation of the patella is commonly seen in both Warmbloods and Miniature Horses, and it is suspected that the connection is that both the very big and very small horses are more likely to be kept in inadequate space as young horses and don't develop the proper strength in their hindquarters, which predisposes them to stifle issues.

Prevention

In addition to buying and breeding horses with good stifle conformation, ensuring your young horses have lots of space and varied terrain to run and play on will set them up to have good, strong hindquarters. Avoid keeping young horses in stalls as much as possible, and turn them out with playmates to encourage them to be active.

As your horses mature, particularly if they've shown a tendency to lock their stifles, working with them with a focus on building hind-end strength and balanced movement will help prevent the development of issues. Stalling, even in older horses, can cause a flare-up of the issue.

Treatment

When the joint doesn't unlock readily after a horse has walked a few steps, you can try backing him up to help. Generally, this allows the patella to move back into place, and if it doesn't, sometimes startling the horse will allow it to unlock. If the joint just won't unlock, or you see it happen a lot, you definitely need to have a vet examine your horse.

Work closely with your vet to make a plan. In most cases, a combination of maturity and a focus on building hind-end strength gradually reduces the frequency of the locking until it goes away entirely. It can return, however, when a horse has a reduction of fitness or a change in management (such as a return to stalling).

If exercise and maturity don't show any improvement, there are surgical procedures that can help, which you should discuss with your veterinarian.

Dwarfism

Because the Miniature Horse is a "size" breed, early breeders were more concerned with size than anything else. Whenever you breed for a single trait at the expense of everything else, you're bound to find some undesirable outcomes. With

8.2 *A dwarf is much smaller than an average Miniature Horse, with distinctive deformities.*

Miniature Horses, it was dwarfism (fig. 8.2). Because of their tiny size, dwarfs were used as breeding stock in an effort to downsize the offspring, and the genes were passed along. Today, even with decades of careful breeding, dwarfs can pop up in even the most careful breeding programs, though genetic testing is beginning to take the guesswork out of the equation.

Unfortunately, there are unscrupulous breeders and uneducated enthusiasts who think that the tiny size of dwarfs is desirable, and it is not uncommon for them to fetch top dollar at some exotics auctions. Dwarfs are tiny, but they have a myriad of health concerns due to their genetic disorder. They require a lifetime of careful care, are prone to painful joint issues, and have a dramatically shortened life expectancy. Dwarfs are not the right choice for a newcomer to horse care.

Signs of Dwarfism

Dwarfs generally have shortened limbs and neck, a distended abdomen, and a domed forehead. Their nostrils tend to be too far up their face, and they are prone to angular limb deformities, sometimes very severe. An underbite is very common. Some horses show minimal signs of dwarfism, but even these should not be bred to avoid producing a dwarf.

Types of Dwarfism

There are four identified and testable types of dwarfism in Miniature Horses, though there could still be more to discover. One of these results in mid-term abortion, but the other three can produce viable foals with dwarfism. The currently identified strains are all recessive, which means that they need to have a copy of a dwarfism gene passed on from each parent in order for the dwarfism to be expressed.

Health Concerns

In addition to the obvious issues of painful and eventually arthritic joints as a result of the limb deformities, a dwarf has an increased risk of developing breathing issues due to the deformed head shape and nasal cavities, as well as systemic problems caused by squishing normal sized organs into a small body cavity. Dental care is also a concern, with, as previously mentioned, a severely undershot jaw being a very common symptom that can cause issues with eating and dental maintenance.

Dwarfs have a dramatically abbreviated life expectancy, and their quality of life must be carefully monitored. While dwarfs are known to be quite docile and friendly, it is not uncommon for people to mistake their good nature for the fact that they are simply not well enough to protest or move away.

Despite their myriad health concerns and a common misconception to the contrary, dwarfs can get bred, their foals will also be dwarfs, and delivery will be hugely dangerous for them. There should be no possibility of pregnancy.

Prevention and Testing

In the past, breeders' efforts to avoid producing a dwarf foal were limited to careful breeding of only those horses without any dwarf characteristics and hoping for the best. When dwarfs were produced, depending on the breeders, they would either not repeat the cross, or remove one or both horses from their breeding program.

Today, we do have the option of testing for the known dwarfism genes, which allows us to make more educated breeding decisions. If you get your results back and your horse is positive for one of the mutations, that doesn't necessarily mean you have to automatically eliminate the horse from your breeding program if there are lots of other desirable characteristics. What you will have to do is only ever cross with horses that are also tested and are negative for the any of the mutations. This way, you can be assured that your foal won't be a dwarf. If you know that your foal has one parent that is a carrier, it'll be necessary to test the foal as well, as the carrier parent will pass on that recessive gene 50 percent of the time and you'll need this information for future breeding decisions.

Testing for the dwarfism mutations is still a relatively recent development, but more people are starting to test, and more horses being advertised as N/N for the dwarfism panel. Testing is done through the University of Kentucky and will give you a lot of peace of mind when making your breeding decisions.

Tough Decisions

Should you have a dwarf foal born, you have a responsibility to ensure the horse has as pain-free a life as possible. Depending on the severity of the deformities, many dwarf foals are euthanized at birth, while others survive for only a few months

Miniature Tales
Bernadette and Thumbelina

(By Peter and Terry Holt,
Hollyhock Meadow Miniatures)

8.3 Thumbelina is a very carefully cared for dwarf and she works as a therapy animal with Hollyhock Meadow Miniatures.

Early breeders of Miniature Horses sometimes used dwarf stallions to obtain shorter horses. The foals were often very correct but three to five generations later, a dwarf could appear. Both Bernadette and Thumbelina probably resulted from this practice. Many breeders would have had such horses euthanized, but we decided to consider them gifts, never to be sold, and only to be put down should we see that they were suffering. We knew that they would be great pets and great pet therapists.

Both Bernadette and Thumbelina had difficult starts and for several weeks it was questionable if they would survive.

Bernadette was born in May 1998 to a mare called Blue Velvet. She could not pull her tongue in fully; it got sunburned and was sore enough so she could not suck. We had to milk her mother and carefully syringe-feed the milk. After about a week of this she kicked out at one of our visitors and sucked her very cooperative mother. We knew that she was on her way.

Bernadette had what AMHA called "dwarf-like characteristics" (oversized head, underbite, bowed limbs, pot belly) so was not registerable with AMHA. Our friend, Elaine, who's had a lot of pain in her life, volunteered to foal watch. While watching, she would spend hours with Bernadette, grooming her, talking to her, singing to her, and even hosting a first year birthday party complete with a cake and party hats.

As a result of her bowed legs, Bernadette had difficulty with her hoofs turning in. The vets got to know her and tried various platforms on her feet but shortly abandoned the idea and said that we should just consider that this was Bernadette. She also had difficulty

with bleeding gums, which was helped by monthly injections of a B-complex vitamin.

We noticed that if a horse was not feeling well, Bernadette would be close by, so if one of our horses needed to be at the vet's clinic for a period of time she would go along to keep the horse's spirits up. We also think they enjoyed just letting her wander freely throughout the clinic. This happened on two memorable occasions when our horses required major surgery. From this time on she was called Nurse Bernadette.

We had been told that dwarfs could not get pregnant so Bernadette was free to be with all of our horses. One day when, luckily, the vet was at our place, the vet came running and said to come and help as Bernadette's water had just broken. In disbelief, we scrambled to help. It took three of us to pull out a dead foal, once again a dwarf. Amazingly, Bernadette survived this ordeal. Thereafter, Bernadette was never allowed to be with "the boys."

At age 12, Bernadette had really slowed up. In her last days, she hung around our first foal, Flurry, now a 15-year-old mare, who was ailing. The vet said that Flurry had cancer and that Bernadette was now in pain. We agreed it was best to have them euthanized.

Both Bernadette and Flurry were euthanized on the same day.

There is a song called "Song of Bernadette" written by Leonard Cohen and sung by Jennifer Warnes. Every time we hear that song we shed a tear for Bernadette. Unlike some owners who give dwarfs away, send them to a petting zoo, or have them put down, we looked upon Bernadette as a gift.

In 2008 Thumbelina, another dwarf was born (fig. 8.3). Although her parents were both black and white, she is a palomino pinto with light blue eyes—close to an albino. Her mother Trudy was an oversized Miniature and her father an AMHA-registered stallion with a multitude of offspring. Thumbelina also had sucking difficulty and, like Bernadette, required syringe feeding for some time. Her skin was so fair that she was also subject to sunburn. We had to improvise a bug mask to shade her sensitive face and keep her out of the sun as much as possible. While clearly a dwarf, Thumbelina was less extreme than Bernadette. Her jaw line and legs were not as incorrect. Thumbelina is now eight years old and just over 24 inches tall at the withers.

We also consider Thumbelina a gift who should be a respected member of our family. She became an early hit with our many visitors but we were quick to tell them that she is a dwarf—not a normal Miniature Horse. She loves to go from person to person undoing their shoelaces. Thumbelina is very mild-mannered so is not a threat to the youngest of people. She frequently sneaks into the bath stall when others are being groomed and has no difficulty in trying to be the center of attention—even the largest of horses like her. Thumbelina, however, is quite capable of sticking up for herself and is very intelligent: she knows that if she hangs back when the others are being fed she will get a special handout. She is the only horse allowed in Terry's garden on the promise that she will not eat the strawberries. Like Bernadette, she is potbellied and we are frequently asked if she is pregnant—but we know she is not!

Her right front leg is more crooked than the others with a tendency to throw her hoof out. Initially, the vet tried correction of the hoof with an epoxy build up, however, this was not successful and frequent hoof trims were deemed to be the most effective, so early on we decided that Thumbelina would have a pedicure each month.

Like Bernadette, Thumbelina greets every tour group as the official greeter. Twice every summer she goes to a nursing home for the better part of a week. She clearly remembers the route through the building and anxiously awaits the abundance of apples that fall from the tree in her pen. She has a fenced-off area in their central courtyard complete with a miniature barn. Each year we are told stories of how she makes a difference in the lives of the residents—for example, the man who speaks little but looks forward to spending time with her during her stays. Each day Thumbelina goes on rounds to visit the shut-ins. The first time she went we took her with another Miniature Horse that we thought was mild-mannered. Shortly we had to retrieve him as he was pushing her around, so Thumbelina goes on her own and is quite happy to do so. Being alone is not usually what a horse wants. Each year her picture usually appears in the local newspaper with a different senior!

In our stable Thumbelina also has what we call our Amazon door. It is a door to a stall that is short enough that only Thumbelina can enter. It only took her half-an hour to learn how to use it. She uses it when she needs "quiet time."

While having a dwarf would not be the preference for an expected foal, from our experience you will see that they can become a rewarding part of your herd. They require some devoted attention and will command an audience. You must quickly explain that dwarfs are an anomaly but that they are wonderful gifts.

before their physical ailments become so great that humane euthanasia is the only option. Some, with exceptional care, have a comfortable life for many years. Only you can decide what is right for yours, but it is your responsibility to protect a dwarf from people who don't understand the special needs, and an auction is no place for a dwarf Miniature Horse.

Hyperlipemia

This is most often seen in Miniature Horses, ponies, donkeys, and other easy-keepers. These horses usually become hyperlipemic following a period of stress or anorexia (not eating). Any time your Miniature Horse isn't eating as usual, you need to be very concerned about this possibility and do everything you can to get feed into him while immediately consulting your vet.

Miniature Tales
Rebelle

Rebelle was a bright, curious, and very opinionated mare (fig. 8.4). She'd had a few foals, and all of them were born outside because she hated the barn. When foaling was imminent, she would just pitch an impressive temper tantrum until she was turned outside, and then lie down and foal—on her terms. One year, she lost her foal, a late-term abortion, and though it wasn't a difficult delivery, she did have a retained placenta so was quickly taken to the vet clinic for treatment. The next morning when I got to work at the same clinic, I asked how she was doing as I went back to visit her. "She's doing well," the veterinarian told me, "Seems quiet and resting comfortably, though her heart rate is elevated so we are watching her closely."

As soon as I looked over the stall at her, I knew Rebelle wasn't doing well. Being locked in a stall—a strange stall yet— should have had her in a full tantrum and attempting to charge out the

8.4 *Rebelle was a boisterous and inquisitive personality. Any change in her demeanor needed to be taken seriously.*

door whenever it was opened. Instead, she stood with her head in the corner, a pile of hay at her feet and barely looked my way as I came in. With my report on her usual fiery self to go by, the vet immediately drew blood and found the excess of lipids present.

Despite IV fluids and the best care the clinic could give her, Rebelle's organs began to fail. We had to say goodbye to her.

In response to a stressful event or lack of food, the body's response is to use the fat stores. Hyperlipemia occurs when this process triggers a mass dump of lipids (fat) into the blood stream. When blood is drawn on a lipemic horse, the lipids quickly separate from the rest of the blood, and sit on top, a thick layer of fat. The liver and kidneys attempt to do their job and filter the blood, but the huge amount of lipids are too much for them. Organ failure is the usual cause of death in hyperlipemic horses.

Risk Factors

Overweight horses, as they have more fat accessible to dump into the bloodstream, are more at risk, so maintaining a healthy weight is a good practice. However, hyperlipemia isn't going to spontaneously occur without an additional event. Any time your horse has a traumatic experience—a difficult foaling, colic, for example—or if he simply stops eating for a period of time, you need to be concerned about him becoming hyperlipemic.

Treatment

Immediate veterinary care anytime your horse goes off his feed is critical. Once a horse is hyperlipemic, your veterinarian will put him on IV fluids to try to help flush the lipids out of his blood, but prevention is more effective than treatment. Being proactive and ensuring immediate treatment any time your horse is ADR (Ain't Doin' Right) is the best thing you can do.

PART 3:

Miniature Horse
Breed Shows

Chapter 9:

Making Your Horse Look His Best

Conditioning

Getting your horse to look his best takes a lot more than just grooming on the day of the show. You need to start at least a couple months ahead, with proper feed and exercise to get your horse in peak condition. Obviously, Miniature Horses, in general, are far more likely to be too fat than too thin, and your program is likely going to be geared toward weight loss and fitness gain. Halter horses are best shown fit, but certainly not thin. Though a tucked-up tummy, refined neck and muscled hindquarters are important, the ribs and backbone should not be visible, and too thin shouldn't be confused with refinement.

Good quality grass hay along with a vitamin and mineral supplement is a good place to start, and your ration can be adjusted from there based on your horse's special needs. General good health is important to make your show horse truly shine, so ensure good parasite control and dental care to allow him to get all the benefit of his feed.

Exercise is also important to gain condition and fitness. A well-muscled horse is always going to look more balanced and polished. Depending on your horse's fitness, begin with around 10 minutes of exercise (lungeing, for instance), several times per week and increase as your horse becomes used to the exercise. The amount and intensity will depend on your horse's age and starting level of fitness. Weanlings and yearlings shouldn't do excessive amounts of lungeing as their joints are still forming and don't benefit from the stress of constant turning. After basic fitness improves, many people use sweats, neoprene, and fleece wraps on the neck, throatlatch, withers or belly to tone these areas further. Soft fabric sweats can be left on them in their pen or stall, while neoprene sweats are used during exercise and usually left on for no more than an hour before being removed and the area beneath them rinsed and dried well.

Grooming

Miniature Horses are generally shown body clipped, though it isn't a requirement. They do need to be absolutely polished though, particularly if they are competing in Halter, and it is difficult to get them to have a tight enough coat without clipping. If you do choose to show your

Miniature Horse in full coat, clean up the long hair on his fetlocks, chin and ears.

Body clipping for show is a big undertaking, and if you have never done it, you'll probably want to do your first clip well in advance of the show to practice.

Deciding If and When to Clip

Clipping can loom as a pretty big deal to anyone who wants to show a horse. In warm climates, it may be advisable to body clip for your horse's comfort, and sometimes it's just nice to clean him up and have him looking his best.

Your horse will shed out on his own, though Miniature Horses can be slow. I like to joke that they are always shed out to their summer coat by the end of July, just in time to start hairing up the first week of August. But you definitely shouldn't feel like you automatically have to body clip your horse. If he is happy and healthy, well-groomed in general, you certainly don't need to clip him.

Generally though, if you are going to show a Miniature Horse, you're going to want to body clip him. Depending on your horse's color and your personal preference, clip from two to seven days prior to the show. Competitors who are serious about Halter will re-clip for every show of the season.

Anytime you choose to clip off your horse's natural coat, regardless of the reason, it becomes your job to keep him warm. In my local climate, I put a blanket on clipped horses at night regardless of the time of year, for at least a month. When you are clipping early or late in the year, think long and hard about what blanketing and housing situations you have in place to keep your horse comfortable. When you would not be comfortable walking around outside in a T-shirt at two in

Clipping Needs List

- Clippers (Andis®, Oster®, Wahl®, and Double K® are good brand names)
- Blades (new or freshly sharpened, size 10 or 15 for clipping body, 30 and 40/50 for face)
- Clipper oil
- Clean horse (!)

the morning, it is too cold for your clipped horse to be out without a blanket.

Clipping also leaves a horse more vulnerable to insects and more likely to get sunburned. By choosing to clip, you are also taking responsibility for keeping him safe from these irritants. Fly sheets and masks, fly spray and sunscreen, particularly on white face markings, are likely going to keep you busy.

Start with a Clean Horse

One of the best things you can do to set yourself up for clipping success is make sure your horse is clean. Dirt in your horse's coat not only makes it nearly impossible to get a smooth clip, it is very hard on your clipper blades. Clipping a dirty horse just isn't worth it.

"Do a general clip in the spring as it gets rid of all the winter yuck and hair then your first show clip will be so much easier."

Peggy Tilleman, Ramblin Ranch

9.1 Bathing is a common way to clean your horse in preparation for clipping, but isn't recommended when he has a thick winter coat.

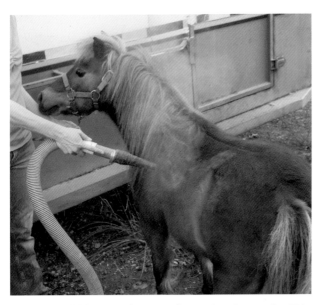

9.2 A livestock blower works very well at getting dirt out of a thick coat, and horses adapt to the noise and sensation quite readily.

Pre-Clip Bath

A bath is a common way to get a horse clean provided you have the facilities and/or climate for it. Get your horse wet with warm water, scrub right down to the skin with a horse shampoo, and rinse a lot (fig. 9.1). When you are dealing with a winter coat, a bath can be much more challenging: sometimes the coat is so thick that it can be nearly impossible to get the horse wet right to the skin, let alone get the dirt out. Then it can take forever to dry, and be difficult to keep the horse warm, comfortable, and clean in the meantime. While I have had good luck clipping wet on a shorter coat, with thick winter hair you'll want it to be dry before you start clipping. You can finish your bath with a spray of a silicone-based coat polish and detangler, which can also help the clipping blades slide through the coat.

Livestock Blower

Using a powerful blower designed for grooming cattle and other livestock is an excellent way of cleaning a coat before clipping (fig. 9.2). Slowly give your horse a chance to get used to the noise and sensation of the blower; most horses quickly discover it's not as scary as it initially seems, and some really enjoy it. Get very close and blow against the grain of the hair to ensure you get all the dirt and dust out of the coat—you'll be able to tell if the horse is clean when the clouds of dust stop appearing. Pay close attention to right along the topline as that tends to be the dirtiest part. Since you're blowing the dirt out, it will settle on other parts of your horse, so to really get him clean enough to clip, you'll have to go over him a few times.

Using a blower is much more efficient than

bathing, particularly with a winter coat, as you can then start clipping immediately, instead of having to wait until it dries, which can easily be the next day.

Livestock Vacuum

A vacuum works similarly to a blower, but instead of blowing the dirt out of the coat, it suctions it out. As with the blower, be sure to allow your horse to get accustomed to the noise and sensation at his own pace, and pay close attention his back, where the most dirt tends to hide.

No matter which method you choose to get your horse clean, it isn't a step you'll want to skip. A clean horse is a vital ingredient for an attractive clip job.

Choosing Clippers and Blades

A lot of people just starting out with Miniature Horses think that their pet grooming clippers or the ones they've used for years to do bridle paths on their full-sized horses will be sufficient. Body clipping a Miniature Horse is a whole new

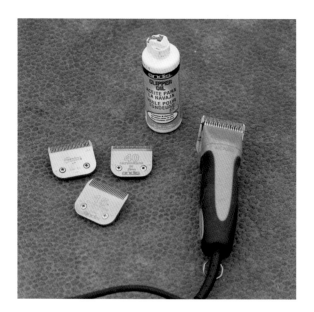

"I would have to say the cleaner the better for any Miniature Horse but for shows especially! A body clipped and braided horse (I mostly go to Combined Driving Events) shows respect for the event and the judge. Your Miniature Horse will stand out negatively if not immaculate in his turn-out according to the discipline you are in."

**Brenda Glowinski,
Glowinski Miniature Horse Supplies**

ballgame, and it is worthwhile investing in a set of clippers powerful enough for the job (fig. 9.3). Some good brand names are Double K®, Oster®, Wahl®, and Andis®. You don't need the full-sized livestock clippers generally, and while they can be good for the body, you'll want another, smaller set for the legs, head, and ears anyway, so getting a smaller set that can do everything is probably going to be the most economical. I really like my Andis Excel 5-Speed clippers: they are small, light, and quiet, but powerful enough to cut the heaviest winter coat without an issue.

When you are clipping for your own preferences or your horse's comfort, a size 10 blade is sufficient. Most often, I use a 10 to body clip for show as well, but someone who is serious about Halter competition will body clip with a 15 or 30 blade instead. Deciding which to use will depend on your horse's coat and color, and your management system. Remember that, as I've already mentioned, when you take away your horse's natural

9.3 Having the appropriate equipment available will make your job much easier: a good set of clippers, a couple sharp blades, and clipper oil.

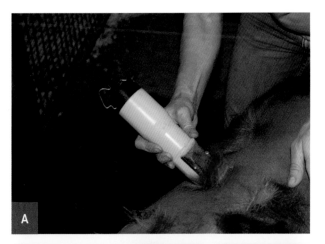

A

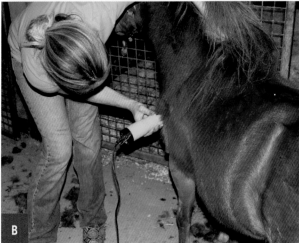

B

C

9.4 A–C Clip against the grain of the hair, with a consistent pressure.

"Always show with a fresh clip (a few days old at the maximum). Make sure your bridle path is done fresh for every show. Black hair dye or black temporary spray can help make a dark horse look his best if his mane is sun-bleached."

Kaycee Lunde, Amaretto Miniature Horses

coat, you also take away his protection against cold, insects, and sun, and the closer the clip the more vigilant you'll have to be with blankets, fly spray, and sunscreen.

When you are clipping for show, you'll also want to invest in a 30 and 50 (or 40) blade for close work on the face. Be sure to keep your blades well oiled; clippers come with oil and instructions for use, but you can also purchase oil separately. Good clipper and blade maintenance not only extends the life of your equipment, but it makes the whole process a lot easier. Clipping is hot, hard, dirty work when you have equipment that is well maintained and working correctly, but is even worse when you have blades that won't cut!

Getting Started

Horses, unlike dogs, are clipped against the grain of the coat (figs. 9.4 A–C). Using your 10 blade, or whichever you've decided is right for your situation, begin on the shoulder or hip, and with your clippers on, lay the flat of the blade firmly against the horse. You can tip the blade slightly in the direction you are clipping so that the most pressure is at the cutting edge and take the hair off in smooth, long strokes. A consistent and firm pressure gives you a much smoother clip, and is less likely to tickle and irritate your horse.

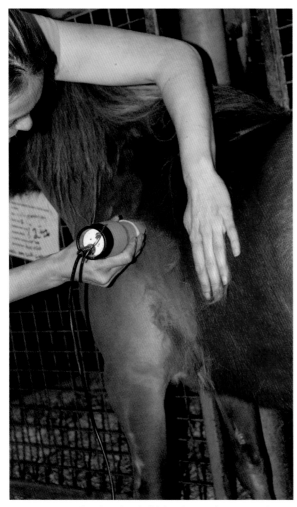

9.6 When you and your horse need a break, don't be afraid to stop midway. A blanket can keep him clean until you've both rested and are ready to try again.

9.5 Using your free hand to hold the skin in place not only makes it easier to clip, it increases the horse's comfort because he will know where to expect the clippers to touch him next.

If you are clipping for the very first time, it is strongly recommended to either clip well in advance of the event you are planning for, or practice clipping a horse that isn't going anywhere. While it isn't technical, getting proficient takes a bit of practice.

Take Your Time

If your horse has never been clipped, he will understandably need some time to understand that while clippers are loud and feel weird on his skin, they aren't painful. Don't get in a fight with your horse, or try to overpower him. Take your time even if it means that all you accomplish the first day is being able to touch your horse with the clippers; making sure that you let him become accustomed to clippers at his own speed will help make future clipping experiences much more positive (fig. 9.5).

If your horse has been standing well and suddenly starts reacting, first check your blade. Clipper blades can get very hot, and it's a good idea to have a couple of blades in each size, so one can be cooling on a damp cloth or ice pack while you are using the other. If your blade isn't hot, then maybe it's just time for a break: your horse won't mind going back in his pen only partially clipped (with a blanket to keep him clean), and things might go a lot smoother later on (fig. 9.6).

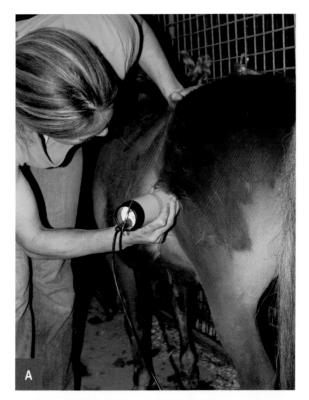

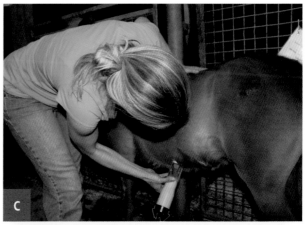

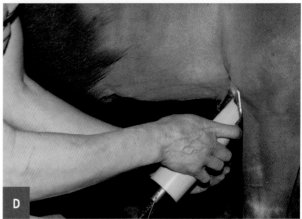

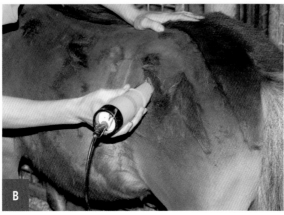

9.7 A–D   The flank can be a tricky spot to get smooth: you need to clip in many directions to stay against the grain of the hair (A & B). Clipping the belly is awkward to reach, however, for safety, it is best to stay on your feet (C). At the elbow and stifle (at the top of the legs) there is a lot of very fluffy hair and very thin, sensitive skin (D). Stretching out the limb can help, or moving the skin, but always be very careful not to cut the horse in this area.

Tricky Parts

For the most part, once horses get used to the sensation and noise of the clippers, they don't mind being clipped on their body and neck, and often even enjoy it, wiggling their noses when you get to a particularly itchy bit. But some spots are more sensitive and they might protest (figs. 9.7 A–D). Having a helper available can make a big difference, as is taking the time to show the horse it is okay. If you have a horse that simply won't allow you to clip his ears or legs or whatever other spot he's decided is just too tickly, don't let yourself or your horse get hurt over it. Talk to your veterinarian about a sedative to make the experience less traumatic.

Ears

Ears are probably the most common part that horses don't like to have clipped, and really you can't blame them (fig. 9.8). In addition to the increased noise of the clippers, there is a very real risk of poking or cutting them with the clippers, so be cautious. Deciding how much hair to take is again going to be up to you—show groomers would tell you that the insides of the ears need to be clipped with one of your closest blades. For my horses that live outdoors 24/7, I feel much more comfortable just trimming off the hair that sticks out of the ear until it looks neat and tidy. When clipping the inside and front of the ear, it is safer to clip with your blades pointing up, as clipping down into the ear is riskier for poking or nicking the ear.

Many people choose to use a twitch to get their horse's ears clipped. A twitch is a clamp or cord that twists or pinches the upper lip of the horse to distract him from the procedure. Pressure in this region is said to release endorphins, which calm the horse. In our herd, when we are going to go this route, we generally just have our helper squeeze the horse's upper lip with her hand, rather than use one of the harsher mechanical devices.

Legs

Lower legs are another place that many horses are touchy about (figs. 9.9 A–D). Lifting the leg

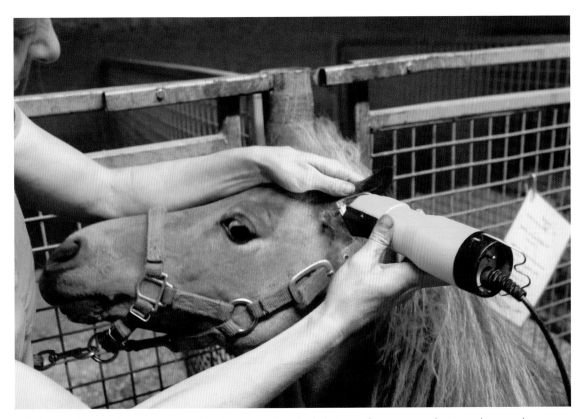

9.8 Ears are the spot that horses are most likely to protest so check that your clippers are not hot, turn them to a lower setting to minimize noise, and be very careful around the sensitive edges of the ear.

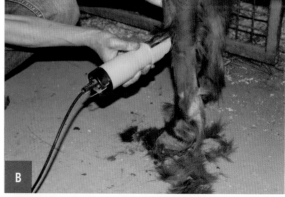

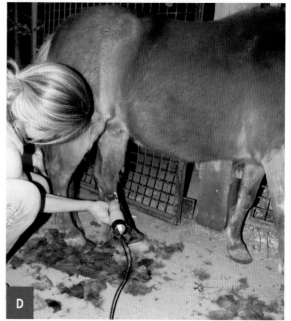

9.9 A–D   Legs can be clipped both on the ground or held in your spare hand, depending on your horse's preference. It is easier to clip the back of the limb—in the pastern and around the ergot—with the limb held by the cannon bone and the hoof relaxed. It is often easier to see the inside of the limb from the opposite side, but watch that you don't startle your horse by touching him with the clippers on a different leg than he is anticipating.

and holding it securely can often make them more comfortable. This is where you definitely want to check your blade temperature often—hot blades on the legs can provoke a dramatic response. Make sure that you keep yourself in a safe position so you aren't caught by surprise by a sudden kick or leap. Again, a helper to hold, scratch, and otherwise distract the horse is a great asset. Remember that making it a good experience, rather than attempting to overpower your horse, will set you up for much more pleasant clipping experiences

in the future. Even though our horses are small, manhandling them isn't fair to them, and can easily become dangerous for us. Though they are small by horse standards, they are very strong and you definitely can get hurt—or worse, they could.

In a horse that is accustomed to clipping, most of the limb can likely be clipped with it on the ground. The back of the leg, with the tendons and fetlock and pastern joints, can be trickier to get a smooth clip. When clipping for a show, a rough clip on the legs can make them look crooked so pick up the leg and hold it in your free hand by the front of the cannon bone, allowing the hoof to relax. This gives you good access to clean the hair out of the back of the pastern and fetlock. Clip away from the ergot (the point of the fetlock) in every direction to get a clean clip.

Make sure you get a nice clean clip around the coronet band, at the top of the hoof. Any straggly hairs left there will make your clip look much less polished, as well as make the application of hoof polish difficult.

Mane and Forelock

Miniature Horses have a lot of mane. It is one of their charms, in many ways, but if you are trying to showcase the fact that they truly are a horse in miniature, that mane can be quite overwhelming and just plain messy.

Begin by cutting a bridle path (fig. 9.10). Find the bony bump between the horse's ears that marks his poll, and use a comb to make a straight part. Clip back from there to create a bridle path, but don't go longer than the length of the ear at first. Comb the mane and stand back to see how it looks. Flip sections of mane to the other side of the neck and look again. You want a bridle path to be the right length to best compliment your horse's neck and head. Remember that you can always take more hair off, but you can't put it back on. By moving hair to the other side of the neck and standing back to look, you can play with different options before you make a final decision and cut the hair off.

Once you've cut the bridle path to the length you feel best suits your horse, the mane will lie better if you take the bridle path at an angle toward the underside of the mane. When your horse has a particularly thick mane, you might want to undercut it quite a bit, taking out some of the bulk of the mane from the underneath side where it won't be visible. Many people also over-cut the mane, trimming in from the side on the top side as well, but I prefer to do a minimum of trimming on the visible side of the mane (fig. 9.11).

9.10 *When determining bridle-path length, err on the side of too short; you can always take more off, but you can't put it back on.*

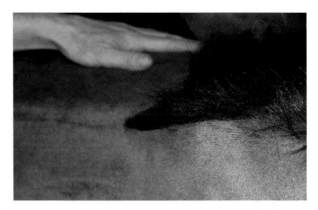

9.11 *Finish the end of the mane by leaving a tidy bit of body hair trimmed in the shape of the base of the mane. Since Miniature Horses are measured at the last hair of the mane, this gives you a buffer to prevent accidentally trimming off the end of the mane and changing your horse's measurement.*

The forelock, as well, can be overwhelming and take away from a pretty face (fig. 9.12). It is almost never okay to trim the length of the fore-lock. Instead, you can reduce its bulk by trimming in from the corners and sides to create a diamond shape. Make sure that the top point of your diamond doesn't go farther forward than the poll, and if you need to take more bulk out, make the diamond smaller from the bottom and sides instead. It is easy to take off more than you intended if your horse wiggles, so once again a helper is useful. It is also a good idea to never trim

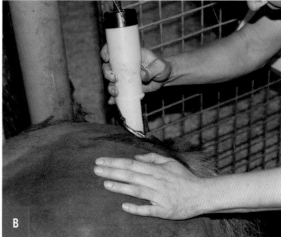

9.13 A & B The top of the tail is traditionally finished in the shape of an inverted V. The size of the V depends on your horse and your personal preference (A). If your horse still has quite a bit of body hair, you may want to use your clippers to shorten or comb out the longer hair. Some people clip the V off in an early clip and leave only the regrowth for a tidier look in their show clip (B).

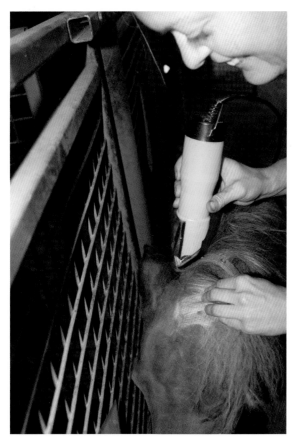

9.12 Remove bulk from the forelock by trimming in from the sides and bottom. Be very careful that a poorly timed "wiggle" doesn't cause you to accidentally clip off the whole forelock.

directly toward the forelock to avoid losing it all with a poorly timed head shake.

Tail

The style when clipping a horse for show is to finish the top of the tail to a neat inverted V shape (fig. 9.13 A). The size of the V is up to your personal preference, but it should be tight against the sides of the tail and come to a neat point in line with his backbone so that it is nice and straight. Some people use chalk to give themselves a line, or loop a piece of string around the dock of the tail and hold it, even tape it, at the middle of the backbone to give a straight guideline to clip along.

In my experience, the most important part of getting a nice straight tail V is to have the horse standing square, and not to fiddle too much trying to make it perfect. The more you try to tweak it, generally, the worse it gets.

If your horse still has a winter coat, you don't want to leave your V with long fluffy hair on it. If it's very hairy, you can carefully clip with the hair to shorten it some. For a less drastic approach, use a clipper blade on its own to comb through the hair and more gradually thin and shorten the hair (9.13 B).

Facial Clipping

Close clipping around your horse's face will highlight his pretty features for the judge (figs. 9.14 A–D). At the very least, your horse needs to have his whiskers and muzzle trimmed the morning of the show with a close blade, a 40 or 50. Generally, horses entered in Halter will also have

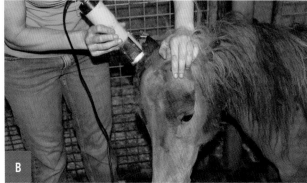

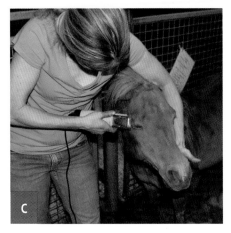

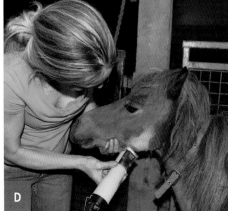

9.14 A–D Clipping the face is easiest if you remove the halter and leave it around the horse's neck so you still have control. Remember to clip against the grain of the hair, be very cautious around your horse's eyes, and take your time to get a smooth clip to show off your horse's pretty face. Some horses, especially those in the process of losing their caps (baby teeth), are very sensitive to the vibration of the clippers on their jaw.

their eyes clipped with the close blade, and it is common practice to shave the muzzle and over the eyes with a razor. This sort of facial sculpting requires lots of practice to do well, and it's better to just use the 50 blade and blend well than it is to have a poorly done razor shave. If you do want to be able to groom to this level for Halter, I recommend learning from someone with a lot of experience and spending time practicing long before a show. My personal choice is not to use a razor on my horse's face, but it is the standard practice in the Halter ring (fig. 9.15).

9.15 First Knights Ohh La La, owned by Marj Brown, has a beautiful face, highlighted by a close shave, or "facial," on her muzzle and eyes.

As mentioned, anytime you clip or shave your horse's face, you need to be aware it is much more likely to get burned in the sun, particularly on any white markings. Application of sunscreen—we use a children's sport brand—will help mitigate this risk.

The body clip can truly transform your Miniature Horse! It is fun to see the glamorous version of the "furry pony" emerge (figs. 9.16 A–C).

9.16 A–C Before...what came off...and after!

Pre-Show Bath

Before the show, your horse needs a bath. If you have access to warm water at your barn, it can save a lot of time to bathe your horse at home first, but most shows have a wash rack with heated water for you to use if you don't have a good option for bathing at home. Wet your horse all over with a warm water hose, making sure to soak right through his mane and tail. Get a clean pail and put a generous squirt of horse shampoo in it before filling it with warm water. Start by dunking the tail in the soapy water and giving it a good scrub then do the same with the mane. Dump the rest of the diluted shampoo on the body and use a soft rubber curry, scrub brush, or your fingers to give the whole body a good scrub. Add a little straight soap on the mane and tail if you feel they need it, and use a whitening shampoo on any white markings to make them really sparkle. White socks will need a proper scrub with the whitening shampoo. We have found that blue Dawn dish soap is very effective for getting white clean and sparkling, and it is safe for horses as it is used on affected wildlife after an oil spill (figs. 9.17 A–C).

Once you've scrubbed everything that needs scrubbing, rinse very well (fig. 9.18 A–C). An attachment on your hose with a bit of pressure helps ensure that you get all the soap out. Soap residue left behind not only attracts dirt and makes the horse appear dirty quickly, but it makes

9.17 A–C Wet the horse down to the skin (A). Use extra soap on socks and other white body markings. Socks will need lots of scrubbing (B). It works very well to dunk the tail in a pail of soapy water, then scrub it (C).

"When putting on hoof color for black hooves on a light coated horse I always put on a layer the night before in case there's any disasters you have time to fix it up."

Meabh Breathnach, Oakwood Stables

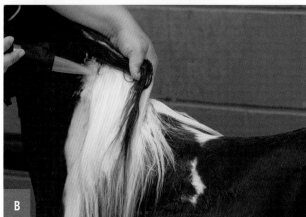

9.18 A–C Be sure all the shampoo is rinsed out of the coat. Rinse, rinse, and rinse some more.

him very itchy and uncomfortable. Rinse and rinse until you are sure there is no soap left, double-checking the mane and tail. Stand back and be certain there are no spots that need a second scrub, especially white markings.

Once you're sure the horse is clean, you can use the conditioner to make the hair silky and shiny. Again, use a clean pail (rinsed of soap) and give a generous squirt of the conditioner before filling it with warm water. Dunk the mane and tail, then slosh the rest over the horse's body and give it a bit of a rub to make sure you got it everywhere. Once again, rinse, rinse, rinse!

Use a sweat scraper to get the excess water out of the coat, then a towel to dry him, especially to prevent his legs from getting cold, and so dirt doesn't stick to him walking back to his stall (fig. 9.19).

Using a silicone-based coat spray such as Absorbine® ShowSheen® helps to make the mane and tail easier to comb out, as well as keeps dust and dirt from sticking to the coat. Use it generously on white markings, which will make any marks or manure stains the horse might acquire prior to show time much easier to clean off.

Brush his mane and tail smooth, and when he

has a white tail, it's a very good idea to braid it and put it in a tail bag to keep it clean.

A spandex hood or bodysuit is the best way to both keep your horse clean until it's time for the show, and to get his mane to lie nice and smoothly (fig. 9.20). When your horse is nearly dry, put on the spandex hood, taking care to make sure that the mane is lying perfectly flat. If the mane is messed up when the hood goes on, you could have quite an unorthodox hairdo by morning when his class goes in the ring.

Show Polish

Your horse's feet need to be polished in some way prior to his class, either with black hoof polish or well buffed and cleaned if they are going be left bare or polished with clear polish (fig. 9.21). Unlike some breeds, it is acceptable to put black polish on white feet if that is what you decide looks best. Sometimes leaving white feet without black polish can give the appearance of a little more

"A really wide black sharpie felt pen can be used to fix scuffed hooves if you don't have time to repolish the hoof."

Pip Breckon

length of leg, but the feet will need more preparation to make them look good enough for the show ring. Start during the horse's bath and scrub them with a grooming block to take any stains off. Feet can also be lightly sanded with a fine grit paper to smooth any ridges. If your horse has stripes on his hooves, check that they are straight—sometimes an off-center stripe can make the whole foot look crooked and you might want to cover it with some black polish instead.

When using black polish, be aware it can—and will—get on everything. Wear gloves, have the horse's tail braided up out of the way, and

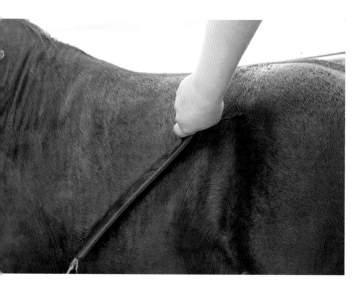

9.19 Use a sweat scraper to remove excess water from the coat before towel drying.

9.20 A spandex hood or bodysuit keeps manes and coats clean and smooth until show time.

get a helper to encourage your horse to stand. Have hoof-black remover on hand, as well as baby wipes, which do a surprisingly good job of removing accidental hoof-black smudges from white socks. Make sure your horse stays still until the hoof black dries, or he will touch his opposite leg with the black, or get shavings stuck to the polish, or any number of other inconvenient messes. Nail-polish drying spray does work on hoof black, so if your horse tolerates a spray well, it can be a good option.

When you remove your horse's blanket to get him ready for his class, you hope he is looking clean, shiny, and polished. Brush his mane and tail and use a rag to clean off any shavings dust. When the top of his tail doesn't lie smoothly, you can dampen it and wrap it for a few minutes to get the little hairs to lie down, and keep everything as slick as possible.

There are a myriad of products for final show-ring grooming. Use a clear or black shine makeup for the horse's muzzle and over his eyes, and gel on his forelock and mane to keep everything smooth and in place. A coat spray can give him an enhanced shine, and then all he needs is a show halter, an equally well-groomed handler and he is ready to strut his stuff.

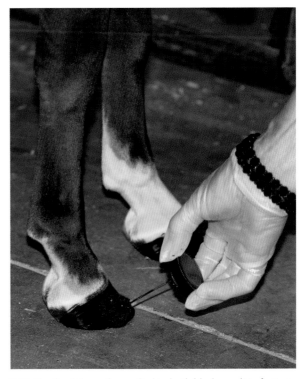

9.21 Hoof polish can be applied to both black or white feet, depending on what preference.

Chapter 10:
Competing

Show Appeal

One of the most popular activities for people to do with their Miniature Horses is showing in the breed ring, or in open shows. Showing appeals to people for a variety of reasons: maybe you love the competitive nature of breed shows—Miniatures have a show circuit in two main registries that is every bit as competitive as any other breed of horse. Or it could be you like having a goal to work toward as you're training your horse, and entering a new class in your local show could give you something fun to practice. Perhaps you enjoy the camaraderie of the show circuit—where better to find a group of fellow Miniature Horse lovers?

If you are planning to raise foals, it is worth considering showing your horses to see how they stack up. Even if raising show-ring winners isn't necessarily the focus of your breeding program, it is good for both promotion and the opportunity to stand back and truly compare your horse to others, with the added bonus of an unbiased, third-party opinion.

Rules and Registrations

If competing at Miniature Horse breed shows is on your priority list, you'll need a registered horse. It's a good idea to do some research and find out which registry has the most shows in your local area. Generally, a double-registered AMHA and AMHR horse will cover your bases, but it's good to know which registry will give the most options in case a single-registered horse catches your eye.

If you already have an unregistered horse, you won't be able to show in sanctioned shows, but that doesn't mean that you can't show. Most local shows will accept Miniature Horses in Halter, Showmanship, and In-Hand Trail classes, and might be willing to offer more classes if entries warrant.

When researching, if you find your local area has mostly AMHA shows and you have an AMHR registered horse (or vice versa) there is a "hardship-registration" option. If your horse meets the requirements, you can pay a fee to get him registered in the other registry. Contact the registry or read the rulebook for specifics.

Your horse's registration must be up to date (permanent papers for horses over three years of age, gelded status up to date, and ownership transferred).

Youth, Amateur, Open

One of the ways classes are divided is according to handler. Youth exhibitors are 18 years or younger, and, generally, classes are also further divided by age, so younger exhibitors don't compete against the older. Youth exhibitors sign up for a youth card from the registry to collect points toward high point awards.

Amateur classes are for adult exhibitors who do not make money training or showing horses. Check the rulebook of the registry for the special rules, but most exhibitors will fall into this category. Some shows also offer Novice classes for beginner exhibitors, or levels of amateur, to allow newcomers to compete without the experienced exhibitors in the class. AMHA also offers an Amateur Owned Trained and Exhibited class to allow those people who train and condition their own horse to show him in a class without any professionally prepared horses.

Open classes are, as the name implies, open to everyone. Amateur, Youth, and Professional are all able to enter. At the biggest shows, Open classes will be the most competitive and heavily populated with professionals, but at smaller shows it can be an opportunity for everyone to show together (fig. 10.1).

A wide variety of classes are available, which means that you'll certainly be able to find an area in which your horse will shine! The following is a description of each type of class you can compete in, as well as information about how to prepare your horse and yourself for the competition.

Halter & Showmanship

Halter Classes

Halter classes are the beauty pageant of the horse world. This is where your grooming, conditioning, and training come together to showcase the quality of your horse.

While the foundation of a good Halter horse is correct conformation, his fitness, grooming, and especially his "sparkle"—his willingness to show for the judges, is what is going to give him the winning edge. Miniature Horses are shown similarly to Arabians, and a Halter class is a performance.

What Your Horse Needs to Know

Horses are expected to walk, trot, and stand and pose for the judge. In AMHA, any potential breeding animals (mares and stallions) must also show their teeth. Horses are led on your right side, part of a very old tradition of always working with

10.1 At a Miniature Horse show you find people of all ages and experience levels competing and having fun.

10.2 A & B One of your first chances to make a good impression on the judge is with a nice forward trot (A). A horse that stands well and really performs in a halter class is always more competitive than one that doesn't (B).

horses on their left. Historically, most people being right-handed, and swords carried on the left hip for easy access, would've made mounting on the right side of the horse quite challenging. Even though Miniature Horses are a unique and modern breed, the traditions of horsemanship carried down through the generations still do have a strong influence.

Practice makes perfect! Just because a horse leads on a halter does not make him ready for a Halter class. Your horse needs to walk beside you on a loose line, trot willingly to show off his movement, and stand and "show." Generally, the walking comes pretty easily, it's the trotting and standing that takes a little work. If you'd like to be prepared with exactly what is expected of you, the general Halter class pattern is outlined in the rulebooks.

Sometimes, a helper to give a bit of a chase is necessary to get a good trot going, until your horse gets the hang of it. Be sure to stay back beside your horse, at his shoulder. Horses don't take well to being dragged behind you, and, without you in front of him, he is far more likely to give a good big trot. Push forward with your right hand on the

lead rope 6 to 8 inches from the halter, cluck or give whatever voice command you have chosen to tell your horse to speed up, and "trot" yourself. A whip in your left hand to touch his bum as you do this will help when you are cueing to trot, but I find another person works far more easily and is less worrisome for your horse. I've also had excellent results from teaching the horse to touch a target, and using that to encourage him to trot along with me.

As always when working with horses, repetition and short, frequent training sessions are more effective. You want a nice, free, forward trot to show off your horse's movement, and it's one of the first things the judge will see so it's a good chance to make a positive impression (fig. 10.2 A). A horse that won't trot, drags, or stalls isn't going to be shown to his best advantage.

Standing and showing is a large portion of the Halter class (fig. 10.2 B). Horses are shown "square," with the front feet and hind feet even with each other and all four legs perpendicular to the ground in AMHA, and slightly stretched or "parked" in AMHR. Horses that are excessively stretched, with the hind feet out behind, will be asked by the judge to re-set correctly. The horse's feet can be positioned using cues from the halter, or they can be "hand set." Unlike in Showmanship class, where you would not be allowed to touch your horse, in Halter, you may pick up and place each foot, but excessive time spent physically moving each foot may be a detriment to your horse's performance.

The first step to developing a show stance is to teach your horse "whoa." A horse has to stand without moving his feet for a long period of time, and this is the most important thing you can teach. Once he will stand, start having him stand with his feet where you want them. I find it's easiest to walk him into position so that the right hind foot is where you want it to be, then set the other three feet around it, beginning with the left hind and then the front feet. This is easy to say, but it takes time and patience to get it right. Only once the horse is comfortable with having his feet placed, and with standing still on a loose lead with you well in front of him, do you start getting him to "show."

Halter classes are all about getting your horse to look his best. A large part of this is getting him to "show," putting his ears forward and stretching his neck to his best advantage. The horse needs to stand squarely on his feet, not leaning, and stretch his neck up and out with his ears up. Obviously, the easiest way to get this result involves treats— find out what your horse likes best! Sometimes a combination of treats and something that makes a noise will get his attention, but you don't want to overuse anything in practice because it won't

be so interesting in the show ring. I've had good luck using both loose oats (feed just a few at a time throughout the class to keep him interested, but not enough so he gets distracted by chewing), and large "crunchy" treats (let him taste but be careful not to let him get hold of one or you'll lose his attention for a long time while he chews). Getting the expression without him leaning is an art, and it takes practice to keep him rocked back and standing squarely on all four legs.

Throughout training your horse to "show," a second person to look at the horse in profile and tell you when he is looking best is very useful. This helps you, from your aspect, learn how to position him so that he is presented to his best advantage, which is your goal in Halter classes. Failing this, setting your cell phone on a nearby fencepost and recording a brief video can give you the chance to see how you are looking and adjust accordingly.

Some horses have a natural affinity for the performance of a Halter class. They can "turn it on" and sparkle for the whole time they are being judged, enhancing their beauty. Other horses— don't! Regardless of conformation and grooming and training, there are some horses that simply don't enjoy the game, and they will never place as well as a horse that does.

What to Wear
You do want to dress up for the show ring, but how formal you get depends on the show. A Championship, or an evening Futurity or Grand Champion class will be formal, while formal wear would be inappropriate at a local show in the morning.

Clean, well-fitted clothing is more important than spending your whole paycheck for the best, most "blinged-out," brand-name show clothes.

Dress pants and a blazer in a color that complements your horse is a good place to start. If you're working on a budget, thrift stores and second-hand stores are great places to find show clothes, and there are Facebook groups and other online resources where people buy and sell used show clothes.

Make sure that whatever you choose to wear, you are comfortable running, bending, and moving (fig. 10.3). You want to be sure that what you wear is going to complement your horse, not distract the judge. Be aware of flapping sleeves, too,

10.3 Your show clothes should present a pretty picture with your horse, and be comfortable enough for your move easily.

Miniature Tales
Sportsmanship

When I was about eight years old, I was already a pretty experienced exhibitor of Miniature Horses (fig. 10.4). At that point though, I was little, cute, and pigtailed, and often won based on my big smile more than my skill as a handler. In one particular case, I was in a Youth Showmanship class, a class that I was accustomed to winning—and I didn't. As could be expected, I was quite upset about it, and I distinctly remember my grandma sitting me down on the tack box and telling me that I was going to march right over to the girl who won the class and give her my congratulations.

The girl who won was much older, and the truth is I never would have gone over to her if my grandma hadn't insisted.

My reluctant, "Hi Lynn, congratulations, you did great in showmanship," was greeted with a huge smile and genuine appreciation. I was startled to discover how pleased she was that I had taken the time to come over and recognize her

10.4 The author and her first show horse, FWF Prancer, with her awards from the 1988 show season.

win, and still remember her expression quite clearly. The experience stuck with me and I think of it often. Regardless of whether I feel the winner of the class is the right choice or not, I don't have the right to ruin it.

Showing horses—and grandmothers—can teach children many life skills; sportsmanship is just one of them, but it is an important one.

10.5 A–C Sherry Wilson McEwen and Lombard's Redi To Be Royal Canadian demonstrate a crisp, smooth haunch turn in a showmanship pattern (A). Sabrina Langner and Imprint Totally Rich and Famous discuss their pattern with the judge following their class (B).

short pant legs, and an embarrassing gap between your pants and shirt that can inadvertently display your undies when you bend over.

Clothing with an easily accessible pocket is also a consideration as this will make it much easier to keep treats and other supplies near at hand.

Ring Procedure

There is a basic pattern for each registry in their respective rulebooks. The pattern may change slightly depending on the venue, but your horse will be required to walk, trot, and show for the judge. If possible, watch a class before yours so that you can see how the ring is set up at your show. If you are in the first class, or otherwise can't watch a class prior to yours, follow the instructions of the ring steward and don't be afraid to ask for clarification.

If it's your very first time in the ring, politely ask the other exhibitors in the class if you could go in last, so you can follow their lead. They won't mind.

Showmanship

One of the few classes that is nearly universal in the entire horse world is Showmanship. Whether you did 4-H growing up or have shown another breed of horse, chances are you have some familiarity with Showmanship. Even if you've shown other animals, the execution might be different but the concept is the same; instead of your animal being judged, you are being judged on your ability to showcase your animal.

In a Showmanship class, you are asked to perform a pattern with your horse. Your preparation in grooming and training, as well as your turnout and presentation is judged. One of the really great things about Showmanship is that absolutely any horse can become exceptional at it with some patience, time, and training, so you don't need to go out and buy a high-dollar horse with top bloodlines to be competitive.

Showmanship is all about you and your horse working together seamlessly, with straight lines and crisp execution of the pattern. You and your horse need to be polished and precise.

What Your Horse Needs to Know

You will find the standard patterns that you'll see in a sanctioned show in the rulebook for the registry, and the pattern will be posted prior to the class so you can memorize it (figs. 10.5 A–B). The elements that you need to practice will be walking and trotting in straight lines, turning on the haunches, backing, and standing square. In AMHA and any Open shows you attend you'll be expected to use the quarter system during your inspection from the judge. This means that you divide your horse into four quarters and you must stay one-quarter away from the judge at all times. The AMHR uses a half system instead, so you must always be on the opposite side of the horse from the judge.

When executing the pattern, a short pause between each element will make your pattern more precise and allow your horse a chance to rebalance before starting on the next element. Any time the pattern calls for a straight line toward the judge, make sure that it is your horse, not you, that is lined up with the judge or marker, as the idea is that this is when the judge would be able to view how your horse moves. Give the judge lots of space as you approach; you never want to stop so close that the judge feels a need to take a step back, and remember you are going to need to be able to move comfortably back and forth in front of your horse.

Practice changing sides until your horse will stand quietly and you can do so with a minimum of steps. Stay out in front of your horse, as trying to go from shoulder to shoulder is too many steps and will give your horse more opportunity to misinterpret your movement as a cue to move his own feet. Leave some slack in the lead so you don't have to duck under your horse's chin and he can stand nice and straight as you move. Practice the movement until it is smooth and you can do it without thinking so that you aren't worrying about where your feet are, but instead being prompt as the judge moves around your horse.

What to Wear

In a Showmanship class, your horse needs to be well groomed (fig. 10.6). At a local show, a complete halter groom with "razored" face is probably not necessary, but he does need to be absolutely clean and polished. A stray shaving in a tail or a mane that doesn't lie smoothly could be enough

10.6 Taylor Gibbons and Runnin Bare Midnite Cowboy show excellent turnout for a showmanship class.

"I love driving, and the fun of showing Miniature Horses, especially in Halter Obstacle, Driving Obstacle, and Hunter classes. I love the challenge of getting the horse to perform in these classes that really allow the intelligence of the horse to shine."

Dr. Crystal Lee, Burwash Equine Services

to cost you the win in an otherwise excellent performance. Most people turn out themselves and their horses in a Western style, but English showmanship is acceptable as well. A well-fitted Western style show halter or a leather halter without the silver is appropriate for showmanship.

You must wear a hat for Showmanship, as well as boots and—depending on your rulebook—gloves as well. Well-fitted, clean, and matched attire is important. Pants that are too short, untidy hair, or a poorly shaped hat can impact your overall impression with the judge. Because showmanship is a little more formal, especially at the upper levels, a jacket or blazer is more appropriate than a rail shirt. In Showmanship, details like a matching belt and earrings can really add polish to your presentation.

Ring Procedure

At most smaller shows, the entire class is brought into the ring and lined up side by side before doing their pattern one at a time at the direction of the judge. Since most Miniature Horse shows are multi-judge shows, the ring steward will tell you at the gate which judge has been designated as the "call judge" for your class, and that is the judge that you will show to. Just pretend the other judges aren't there, as it is impossible to direct your Showmanship pattern to two or three judges at once.

The judge will acknowledge you and you can begin your pattern. Be sure to smile, and don't be afraid to speak to the judge, especially to return any greeting. Once the inspection is finished, you will be told you can continue and finish your pattern. Don't rush, but be as crisp and smooth as possible. When you return to the line-up and the judge moves on to the next exhibitor, confirm that you are on the correct side of your horse to maintain your quarter (or half).

Remember that you need to continue to show for the entire time you are in the ring, not just during your pattern. If the call judge moves around the ring or comes back down the line for a final look prior to filling out the judge's card, you need to make sure you are paying attention so you can switch sides accordingly.

At large shows, you might enter the ring individually to do your pattern instead of standing in a line-up while everyone else competes.

Performance

One of the great things about Miniature Horses is that they can easily become an all-around horse, competing in many divisions at the same show. Unlike some breeds that have become very specialized, with horses competing in different divisions or disciplines barely resembling each other at all, Miniature Horses are still well suited to compete in many different classes. This means that you can take one well-trained horse to a show and have lots of fun competing in a wide variety of classes, and the next weekend go to a combined driving event, visit a hospital, enter a horse agility competition, or just about anything else you can imagine.

Halter Obstacle

Halter Obstacle is in-hand trail class, and it is a skill that every horse can benefit from working on, even if he never does compete in the show ring. Training your horse to calmly negotiate obstacles improves your partnership and gives you better lines of communication to control the horse's feet and know how to approach new things you may find in your travels. The skills developed in Halter Obstacle are also applicable to Horse Agility.

What Your Horse Needs to Know

Starting with basic Showmanship skills is a great idea before tackling the training for the obstacles themselves. You want your horse to walk, trot, and whoa with you very comfortably, taking his cue from your movement until you are really working together as a team. Obstacles range from traveling over a bridge, tarp, or poles, to backing, side-passing, haunches and forehand turns, small jumps, and ground-tie. The more things you can expose your horse to in preparation, the better.

Being able to move him in any direction calmly and under control is key to a successful obstacle horse. You may need to be able to back, side-pass both directions, and execute a haunches turn all in the same obstacle, so the fine control of each step will set you up for success.

Teach each skill gradually, getting one step at first, and use lots of praise before building on each step to create the whole movement. Because Miniature Horses are small, it is far too easy to get frustrated and start manhandling, chasing, or bullying them, shoving them in the direction you need them to go. Not only will this never win you any ribbons in the show ring, but it is the fastest way to undermine their trust and ruin the partnership you've been building. It is much better to treat your horse as though he weighs 1,200 pounds and pushing him around isn't an option. When your horse isn't responding the way you'd like him to, then he doesn't understand what you're asking and you need to find another way to explain it.

What to Wear

For performance classes such as Halter Obstacle, a rail shirt or a nice Western shirt is appropriate. Obstacle, particularly at local shows, can be a little less formal, but you still need to dress as though you are proud of your horse, and present a professional image to the judges. Make sure what you're wearing is comfortable enough for you to be able to move easily with your horse.

Your horse should wear a well-fitted halter. Most people use a Western style show halter with silver, or a plain leather one, but even a nice new nylon halter would be appropriate. More important is that it fits the horse well so you are able to communicate with him effectively. He should be neat and clean, but he doesn't need to be shined up like a horse in a Halter class.

Ring Procedure

The pattern will be posted at least an hour before the class so you can study it in advance, and immediately prior to the class you will get a walk-through with the course designer and the judges so that you are clear on what is expected. If there is anything that doesn't make sense to you, or if you'd like to clarify an element, this is your chance to ask (fig. 10.7).

10.7 Exhibitors in a Youth Halter Obstacle class walk the course with the judges prior to competing.

ask you to move on to the next one.

Treat an obstacle course like a showmanship pattern. You want it to be a smooth and crisp performance, not just get your horse around the course. Show off your horse's skills and the partnership you've developed through the time you've spent training (figs. 10.8 A & B).

Sometimes at local shows, you determine order of go based on who is willing to go first, but most often at larger shows or championship shows you go in the order in the program or a separate posted order of go. There will be a whistle when the judges are ready for you to start. If you should go off pattern, you'll hear the whistle again, and you'll be disqualified. When you are having difficulty with an obstacle, the judge may

Liberty

In a Liberty class, the horse is turned loose in the arena, while a selection of music chosen by you plays over the loud speakers (figs. 10.9 A & B). You may have one person to help you encourage the horse to show off for a minute and a half, until the music stops, when you must catch your horse within the time limit (1:30 minutes in AMHA, 2 minutes in AMHR) or be disqualified. The horses

10.8 A & B Kimberley Locke and Circle J Bunanza perform a sidepass (A). Emmett Tilleman and Enchanted Acres Shadowfax concentrate on their obstacle pattern (B).

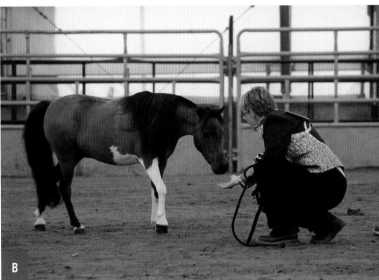

10.9 A & B Hollyhock Meadow Chaps, owned by Karina Van Brabant, performs in a Liberty class (A). Peggy Tilleman and Humm NS Choco Aurora Gem demonstrate a beautiful catch in Liberty (B).

are judged on their performance, demonstration of both trot and canter, use of the whole arena, animation and catch.

Hunter

As in Hunter classes with full-sized horses under saddle, Miniature Horses in Hunter are judged on way of going and form over fences. Unlike full sized horses, they are obviously not ridden (fig. 10.10). Hunter courses contain from six to eight jumps between 18 and 24 inches in height. Horses may trot or canter the course, but consistent maintenance of gait is important, as is a smooth, flowing course and correct jumping form. At the conclusion of the class, all of the horses are asked to trot past the judges to allow them to evaluate their soundness; lame horses will be disqualified. Horses may be braided for Hunter and Jumper and are showing in a Western or English style halter.

10.10 Ramblin Ranch Simply Irresistible shows lovely Hunter form for owner Samantha Birch.

10.11 33.75 inch tall Lucky Four Andys Color Card clears a 36-inch jump in a Jumper Class with Salena LaBine.

Jumper

While a Hunter class is judged on style, in a Jumper class horses must just get over the jumps (fig. 10.11). Faults are assigned for each knock down or refusal, and clear rounds will jump off with the jumps raised. In AMHA, it is strictly a competition over the height of the jumps, and they continue to raise them until a winner is found. In AMHR the jump-off round is timed, and the fastest round with the fewest faults wins. Horses must be carefully conditioned to be prepared to jump the big jumps, but Miniature Horses are excellent jumping horses and, when fit, routinely clear fences that are in excess of their own height.

Driving Classes

There are several different types of driving classes at Miniature Horse shows, so you can find the one that best suits your driving horse. For more information on these, and about getting started in driving, see chapter 11 on Carriage Driving (p. 132). What follows here is a general outline of driving competition.

What Your Horse Needs to Know

In addition to the basic skills of driving, before you get into the show ring make sure your horse is comfortable driving in a variety of locations—around other horses and carts, standing quietly, and backing willingly.

Equipment Needed

The show carts traditionally seen in the show ring are wooden carts with a removable floor and basket to allow the cart to be used for both pleasure and roadster classes. The common brand names are Jerald and Graber. However, particularly at the local level, using a starter metal easy-entry cart or other vehicle is fine as well, provided it is well balanced and comfortable for your horse, as well as clean and in good repair (fig. 10.12).

Show harness can be as high quality and expensive as you could imagine, but any harness that is clean, polished, and fits well and safe is acceptable. It is a rule that driving horses in the show ring must wear blinkers, as well as a side- or over-check. A martingale and/or breeching are optional and can be used as you feel necessary.

It can be easy to be convinced that you need the fancy show cart and harness to be competitive, but your horse is being judged on his performance first. So long as your equipment doesn't detract from that performance, and you make an attractive overall picture, you are fine.

You need to carry a whip in all classes. In the show ring, many people carry a dressage style whip, but if you want to use your whip correctly as an aid, you'll need a carriage driving whip with a lash.

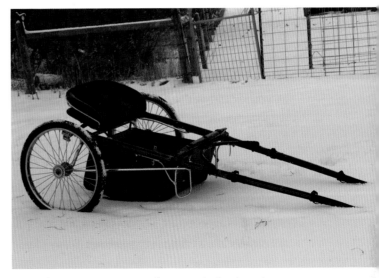

10.12 The most common type of cart seen in the show ring. The basket easily removes to allow the cart to be used in both Roadster and Pleasure Driving Classes.

What to Wear

What you wear depends on the rest of your turnout, your level of competition, and the class you've chosen to enter. From a ball gown (yes, really) in a Single Pleasure Driving class at the World Show, to a nice Western shirt and cowboy hat in Western Country Pleasure at your local show, you'll want to make sure your clothing is comfortable for you to drive in and suits your horse and cart (figs. 10.13 A & B).

10.13 A & B Dale Crocker and First Knight's Shadowfax showing a beautiful turnout for Classic Pleasure Driving (A). Emmett Tilleman and his mother Christine Tilleman in an appropriate turnout for Single Pleasure Driving in a daytime class with Enchanted Acres Shadowfax (B). An evening or championship class may warrant more formal attire.

Just as with a Halter class, it's important your clothing is comfortable for the job that you are doing, so if you're trying on potential driving clothes, be sure you are seated, hold your hands as you would while driving, and make sure that your attire is still comfortable and attractive. Sometimes an outfit that looks great on you when standing becomes awkward when sitting, and it's worth testing it out ahead of time so you know it's going to work.

A hat is appropriate, but not necessary, and you are always allowed to wear a helmet in any class.

Ring Procedure

Driving horses generally get a warm-up prior to their class, either in a separate warm-up ring, or in the show ring. Make use of your warm-up—at local shows it is usually in the show ring, and your horse will have a chance to get comfortable with the ring in addition to warming up his muscles. A warm-up usually takes place in the 10 minutes before the section of driving classes that you find your class, so if you're in the last of a section of six Country Pleasure classes, plan accordingly to take your warm-up before the first class.

Be ready when your class is called. All Pleasure Driving classes enter the ring counter-clockwise, while Roadster classes enter clockwise. The details on what each class is judged on can be found in the rulebook. Follow the instructions of the announcer as you show the required gaits in both directions of the arena, line up at the direction of the ring steward, and back your horse when requested by the judge.

10.14 Once horses are lined up, a header (helper) is required for all Youth drivers, and optional for all drivers. Taylor Hinds Howe drives Smokey Mountain Indian Magic, with header and owner Jodi Crocker.

A "header" (helper) is required for youth exhibitors, and optional for everyone else. Once you are in the line-up, headers may enter and stand near the head of your horse to assist as necessary. Headers should be dressed appropriately for the show ring—they can either be in show clothes, or wearing a white, unmarked smock, and must have appropriate footwear (fig. 10.14).

In Which Driving Class Does Your Horse Belong?
The following guidelines are just that—guides. Depending on their strength and conditioning, as well as the level of competition, horses can often switch from one class to another. There are no cross-entries allowed within one show between the three Pleasure Driving divisions, but you can enter any one of these as well as a Roadster class at the same show.

Horses competing in one of the three Pleasure Driving divisions are shown to a two-wheeled cart with a solid floor. The driver must carry a whip with him.

• Single Pleasure Driving (AMHA) or Pleasure Driving (AMHR) is where the most elevated, collected, and animated horses compete (fig 10.15). Few horses have the talent, strength, and conditioning to be able to be competitive in this class at the elite shows. These horses should be brilliant movers, with the strength to maintain their elevated frame comfortably for the duration of the class. Horses are expected to perform on the rail at the Collected Trot and Working Trot (AMHA) or Extended Trot (AMHR), Walk, and will be asked to rein back. Single Pleasure horses should carry most of their weight on their hindquarter, with light, expressive movement in the front limbs.

10.15 Enchanted Acres Shadowfax in Single Pleasure Driving.

10.16 Lombards Canadian Alacadebra and Joan Cunningham in Country Pleasure Driving.

• Country Pleasure Driving horses don't require the elevation and collection of Single Pleasure horses, but they still show balanced and expressive movement (fig. 10.16). Country Pleasure Driving horses should work in a consistent frame with their hocks well underneath them. They show on the rail at a Pleasure Trot (AMHA) or Country Pleasure Trot (AMHR) and Working Trot (AMHA)

10.17 *First Knights American Idol and Taylor Gibbons in Classic Pleasure Driving.*

10.18 *Lucky Four Andys Color Card and Salena LaBine in Roadster.*

or Extended Trot (AMHR), Walk and will be asked to rein back.

• Classic Pleasure Driving (AMHA) or Western Country Pleasure Driving (AMHR) horses move with long, sweeping strides (fig. 10.17). With a less elevated head carriage and more relaxed frame, these horses should still drive with consistent contact and forward movement. They will

be judged on the rail at a Pleasure Trot (AMHA) or Western Country Pleasure Trot (AMHR) and Working Trot (AMHA) or Extended Trot (AMHR), Walk and will be asked to rein back. Manners are of utmost importance.

• Roadster horses are shown in a two-wheeled cart or roadster bike, with no solid floor and stirrups for the driver's feet (fig. 10.18). Roadster horses are shown at a Jog Trot, Road Gait and full extended Drive On trot. They are not asked to walk, or rein back. Roadster horses are expected to move with speed, brilliance, and animation, with consistent, balanced movement at speed. Roadsters may wear non-weighted bell boots in the ring, and can have their forelock and first section of mane braided with ribbon to match the driver's required roadster silks, a jacket and cap to match (fig.10.19).

10.19 *Roadster drivers wear colored silks, a jacket and cap to match.*

Driving Obstacle

Similar to Halter Obstacle (see p. 121), if your driving horse has the training to develop a careful, quiet temperament, he can begin working on obstacles under harness as well (fig.10.20). Run the same as a Halter Obstacle class, Driving Obstacle horses negotiate such obstacles as patterns around cones, a tarp or bridge, backing, placing a wheel between two poles, pivoting with one wheel in a circle, or transporting items from one place to another. Again, Obstacle needs to be done with a calm, crisp, polished pattern.

Fun Shows

The term "fun show" or sometimes "schooling show" refers to an unsanctioned Miniature Horse show (fig. 10.21). Without the expense of hiring judges who have been carded by the registry, fun shows tend to be more affordable, as well as generally more low key. A fun show can be a great place to start your showing adventure, giving you and your horse a chance to try it out without the investment of show equipment and higher entry fees. Be sure to join your local Miniature Horse clubs to stay up to date on these events.

10.20 Crystal Lee and Excels High C Cruise perform a wheel pivot in Driving Obstacle.

Local Sanctioned Shows

Most regions in North America have some AMHA or AMHR (or often, both) shows. Your local area may be more prevalent in one or the other, or you may have to travel some distance to get to a sanctioned event. Sanctioned shows are generally a little more money to enter, as not only are you being judged by an individual who has been officially carded by the registry as qualified to judge Miniature Horses, but you are also able to gather points toward qualifying for World and National shows, annual high point awards, and lifetime achievements. As they are only open to registered horses, sanctioned shows are a great place for breeders to showcase the horses their breeding program is producing.

National/World Championship Shows

The AMHR National Show and the AMHA World Show are held each fall, as well as regional championship shows. Earning qualification to these shows allows you to compete against the best of the best and vie for the National or World titles. Both these shows are live streamed on the internet, which is a great way to see what they're all about without the expense of travel. Even if you

10.21 *Exhibitors at the Wild N Wooly schooling show learn the finer points of Showmanship from judge Kimberley Locke.*

never do have a horse that you think is ready to compete at that level, or if the show ring isn't how you enjoy your horses, the World and National shows are something to see, with hundreds of beautiful Miniature Horses, as many Miniature Horse lovers, and lots of pomp and circumstance. They're worth a trip, even if you don't bring your horses with you.

Chapter 11:
Getting Started in Driving

Ground Rules

As with any driving horse, getting your Miniature Horse to the point where he is comfortable and confident enough to drive in a show of any kind will take some time, patience, and knowledge (fig. 11.1). If you don't have a solid base of understanding training horses and the correct use of driving equipment, it is strongly recommended you get some experienced assistance with your horse. While driving full-sized horses can be quite dangerous when things go wrong, many people have the mistaken impression that because Miniature Horses are small, they don't need to take the time and care in training that they would with a 1,000-pound horse.

Not only is this not true—you absolutely can get hurt, and perhaps even more importantly, so can your horse—but it is completely unfair to your horse not to treat him with the same respect just because he is less likely to inflict serious harm when he gets scared. Taking shortcuts in his early training might seem to work at the time, but you are setting him up for a very bad experience in the future, when he needs to rely on training that he never got. Horses never forget a bad experience, so even one frightening or painful incident in harness can ruin their confidence forever. It is your job to keep them safe and comfortable.

11.1 Ground driving is just one of many steps in driving training to prepare your horse to be a safe, sane, and confident driving horse.

Green + Green = Black + Blue

A very old saying in horsemanship, it means that a green or inexperienced horse

11.2 A & B Charity Canty and Little Bit Man Among Men participate in a driving clinic with Centered Driving instructor Peggy Brown (A). Morning's Touch of Grace has her harness adjusted by instructor Peggy Brown (B).

combined with a green or inexperienced handler can result in a dangerous situation for everyone.

One of the best ways to get started in driving is to get a very experienced driving horse to help you learn how to drive. There is a lot more to driving than sitting in the cart and holding the reins, just as there is more to riding than sitting on a horse. Even experienced riders can find driving a new and sometimes scary challenge as they are not accustomed to having only their hands and voice to communicate with the horse.

Learning to drive correctly is one of the best things you can do to ensure that driving is a fun and pleasant experience for both you and your horse. Start by taking some lessons: you can usually find a driving instructor with a lesson horse so you can begin learning to drive before you buy a driving horse, making sure it's something you want to invest in further. A beginner-friendly driving horse can be a rare, and, therefore, valuable commodity, not to mention the investment in cart and harness as well.

Driving your Miniature Horse is a great deal of fun for you both, but it isn't something to be taken lightly either. Driving can be dangerous and unless you have the knowledge to properly and carefully teach your horse everything he needs to know, some qualified instruction and assistance is a wiser option than going it alone.

Coach vs. Trainer

A coach or instructor is there to help you with your horse, giving you both the tools to succeed in whatever your goals are. A trainer would train your horse to drive, and teach you the skills to continue to work safely with your new driving horse. Both can be very valuable assistance with driving, or whatever activity you and your horse are embarking on together.

Finding a reputable instructor or trainer in your area will require a little research. Ask lots of people about their experience, and if you find a professional you feel will work, don't be afraid to ask for information on experience and credentials, as well as references from current and past clients (figs. 11.2 A & B).

Any time you are sending your horse to

11.3 *When you want to learn to drive, don't limit your search for an instructor to those who specialize in Miniature Horses.*

another facility for training, ask questions about the standard of care and if at all possible, tour the facility prior to making any decisions. Even when your horse isn't in your direct care, you're still responsible for his well-being and you need to do your due diligence to ensure that the person you are entrusting him to is going to care for him appropriately.

Size Doesn't Matter

When it comes to driving horses, and especially driving horse trainers and instructors, the information isn't size-specific (fig. 11.3). While you may want to find a Miniature-Horse-specific instructor for learning about driving in the breed ring, for the basic information about driving your horse safely, a driving instructor who is certified with your local or national driving organization is your best bet, regardless of what size horses they have. A harness is a harness and a horse is a horse; don't limit your learning based on size.

The more you can learn about harness and how it works, and how to properly communicate with your driving horse, the happier both you and your horse will be, and the more fun you will have together. Learn from everyone you can, take lessons and clinics whenever possible, and always ask why so that you are sure you are doing the right thing for your horse.

Driving Equipment

A big part of keeping you and your driving horse safe is going to be ensuring you have appropriate equipment in good repair.

Harness

There is a wide range of harness available for Miniature Horses, but it can be difficult to find an affordable harness that is comfortable for your horse and sturdy enough to keep him safe. Check the stitching and quality of the leather or synthetic, and recheck it every time you use the harness. The last thing you want is a simple equipment failure to be the reason you and your horse are hurt or scared.

Many lower-end harnesses also aren't built with the comfort of your horse in mind. This doesn't mean they won't be useful in the very early stages of training, but you'll likely want to invest in a better harness before you ask your horse to work in draft—actually pulling the cart. If you're not familiar with harness fit and how each piece functions, be sure to learn all you can, whether from books, videos, websites, or lessons with a qualified instructor. There are many options available, and deciding, for example, whether a breast collar harness or full neck collar is the right one will depend on your situation.

Cart

When shopping for a cart for your Miniature Horse, check that everything is in good repair. Most important is the balance of the cart (figs. 11.4 A & B). In a two-wheeled cart, when the driver is in the seat there should be a very minimal weight on the horse's back. Check by holding the shafts of the cart and having someone else sit in the seat as though she were driving. If you have to hold up the shafts with quite a bit of weight in your hands, the cart is not balanced correctly.

Hitching the horse incorrectly to the cart can also influence the balance of the cart. Once you've found its balance point, make sure that is where the shafts of the cart are set when hitched to the horse in order to keep your horse from having to carry any weight and make everything as easy and comfortable for him as possible.

Miniature Horses are very strong for their small size, and with proper conditioning and a well-balanced cart, can often very comfortably

"How'd I get into Miniature Horses? I was looking for alternatives in the driving world and a way to introduce driving to students who were intimidated by the full-sized horses."

Kathleen Winfield, Doubletree Driving

pull a load twice their own body weight. However, they should not be expected to pull at their peak ability without careful and consistent conditioning and strength-building. Despite their "pit pony" heritage, without proper preparation for the work they are being asked to do, they will be prone to injury like any other horse. Again, if you think you might not have the appropriate knowledge to safely and comfortably hitch your horse to the cart, find a qualified mentor or instructor to help you along the way.

11. 4 A & B A metal easy entry cart is a readily available starter cart for Miniature Horses that is generally safe and well balanced (A). Once you and your horse are ready for more serious driving, you may want to upgrade your wheels, shafts, or the entire cart (B).

Driving Outside the Show Ring

Carriage driving is one of the fastest growing equine sports, and the Very Small Equine (VSE) division is gaining popularity as horse lovers discover the athleticism of the Miniature Horse and the fun of driving. When you drive your Miniature Horse outside the breed ring, you have the opportunity to compete alongside the most diverse group of equines you are likely to find anywhere. In carriage driving competition, a VSE is any equine (including donkeys and mules) under 39 inches or 99 centimeters at the withers, and registration isn't required. If your much-loved Miniature Horse isn't registered, that certainly doesn't mean he can't be a competitive driving horse, and even if your horse is over the 39-inch limit for a VSE, he can compete instead as a Small Pony.

11.5 A & B Katie Iceton drives her pair in a water obstacle at a Combined Driving event (A). Every size, type, and hitch of equine is welcome to compete in Combined Driving, which makes for a very diverse group (B).

Combined Driving Events

Modeled after eventing in the ridden-horse world, Combined Driving was developed in Britain as the ultimate combined test for a four-in-hand of horses. Prince Philip was heavily involved in the creation of the sport. While at the FEI (Fédération Equestre Internationale—the international governing body of all Olympic equestrian sports) level Combined Driving is the realm of the four-in-hand, at the lower levels, it is one of the most inclusive horse sports available. With divisions for every size and shape of driving horse, in every

A

B

turnout—singles, pairs, tandems, four-in-hands—and at every level from Training level for beginner horses or drivers, right up to Advanced and FEI-level competition (figs. 11.5 A & B).

Competition ranges from a less intensive driving trial (Horse Driving Trial or HDT) or an indoor Arena Driving Trial (ADT), to a full, three-day Combined Driving Event (CDE). If you have an interest in this sort of driving (and if you enjoy driving your Miniature Horses, then I absolutely recommend you give combined driving a try!), one of the very best ways to learn about the sport is to volunteer at an event. It requires a lot of people to make these competitions happen, and volunteers are always needed, appreciated, and treated very well. You'll be trained by more experienced people for your job, and have the opportunity to learn about the sport with a front row seat.

Entering a CDE or Driving Trial

Because of the time involved in the sport, events often have a maximum number of entries, and they can fill up quickly. If you are interested in entering, make sure you are on the list for your local event and get your entry in early to assure your spot. All ADS (American Driving Society) approved events are listed in their Omnibus and you are able to see upcoming events in your area there. Non-sanctioned events won't be included, so it is also a good idea to join your local driving club to stay up-to-date on all the local shows and events. Generally driving clubs do a great job of putting on not only competitions, but educational clinics and schooling opportunities, and being a member of your local club is the best way to make sure you're always in the loop.

When you get your entry form for the driving event, you will enter your level (Training,

11.6 The sport of Carriage Driving is rooted in history and tradition, and a beautiful turnout will reflect this heritage. Judith Orr and Toybox Nickles and Dimes make a pretty picture in their dressage test.

Preliminary, Intermediate), your turnout (single, pair, tandem, or team), and your size (for example, VSE or Small Pony). All equines must be at least four years of age prior to competition. In the prize list, you find information about the event to help you prepare, such as which dressage test you'll be driving and how long the marathon will be at your level so you can plan your conditioning accordingly.

Presentation

At most small events and driving trials, "presentation" is judged "on the move" during your dressage test. At a full CDE, your presentation is inspected prior to your test. You are given a score out of 10 (fig. 11.6).

Equipment

Your harness and vehicle need to be clean, polished, and in good repair. They should be well-fitted and appropriate for your horse. Any safe, serviceable harness and vehicle will get you a respectable turnout score, but carriage driving is a sport deeply rooted in tradition, and some of them are still important in the presentation score. Things like having matching hardware on your harness and vehicle, and brown reins versus black, will help bump up your score. There are entire articles and websites dedicated to presentation; it is something you can always learn more about and continue to improve, but starting clean, well-fitted and safe is going to put you in good stead.

Grooming

Your horse also needs to be as clean and polished as you can make him. Because you are showing a Miniature Horse, often the easiest way to get him show ready is with body clipping, but if your horse is shed out well, then cleaning up his legs, ears, and jaw with the clippers would be sufficient. Make sure any white markings sparkle and he is clean and shiny. It is traditional in the driving ring to braid manes, but not tails. Since Miniature Horses generally have a full, long mane, a running

braid is likely the best option. Practice this ahead of time—if your braid isn't going to be nice and even and stay in well, then a well-groomed loose mane is probably a better option.

What to Wear

Dress for Dressage and Cones, as with all aspects of carriage driving, is very traditional. The bedazzled jacket you wear for driving in the show ring would not be appropriate. Your clothing should be quite formal and understated, in complimentary colors with your horse and vehicle to complete the picture. You need to wear a lap robe or apron and your gloves should be brown. A formal hat is generally worn during Dressage, but a helmet is always acceptable.

In Marathon, your clothing needs to be safe but otherwise there are no rules. Many people dress in matching colors and coordinate with brightly colored harness or boots on their horse, or shirts with their team name emblazoned on them. A helmet is required, and a chest protector is recommended for everyone, and required for junior drivers (fig. 11.7)

Dressage

The word *dressage* literally means "training"—it is the demonstration of what your driving horse knows. Your test will be identified in the entry form, and you can download a copy online through the ADS website. This will give you lots of time to practice the elements and memorize it, and you can also walk the test without your horse in the dressage ring at the show any time before

11.7 Lynn Johnson and First Knight's Too Legit To Quit (Mickey) during the marathon portion of a CDE. Bright colors and themes are embraced on marathon day!

the competition starts. Each test will consist of a series of figures and gaits to test your horse's training and your driving skills. You will be scored on each movement by one or more judges (depending on the size and level of the event), and you will get the scoresheet(s) at the end of the competition with your scores and comments from the judge, so you will know what you did well on, and what you need to work on to improve your scores next time.

The standard dressage ring for driven dressage is 40 meters by 80 meters. VSE's usually compete in a ring 30 meters by 60 meters, but might drive in the full-sized ring or in a 20 meters by 40 meters ring. The size should be listed in the entry information, so that you know what size of circles to practice. In Combined Driving, your dressage score is turned into penalty points, so the lower your score, the better you and your horse have done.

At Training level, the tests include a working trot, working walk, and free walk, and you will be asked to halt, and potentially to back up. You will be rewarded for rhythmic gaits, with good relaxation and accuracy. Each test includes circles in both directions, transitions, and a change of rein. When you move up to Preliminary, you'll also have to lengthen the trot, and do smaller circles, half-circles, and other increased level of difficulty.

Your Dressage time will be posted, so you can plan your preparations and warm up accordingly. You will need to go for a safety check prior to your test, and at a big event your time for having your presentation judged will also be posted. The judge will ring the bell when ready for you, and from that time you have 60 seconds to enter the ring. At some events, you can use this time to drive around the perimeter of the dressage ring to let your horse get a look at the area (fig. 11.8).

11.8 *Becky Taylor and Watson during their dressage test.*

When you go off course on your dressage test, the judge will blow a whistle. Go over to the judge to find out where you made your mistake, and where to continue from. You will get a penalty for going off course, but can complete your test and get a score. If you are very worried about memorizing your dressage test, at Training Level you can often have someone "call" your test for you, reading out the movements as you get to them to keep you from getting lost. If you go off course three times, you will be eliminated from the competition, but you still get to participate and get your scores for Marathon and Cones.

Marathon

The Marathon includes distance, as well as speed and precision through the marathon obstacles, or hazards (figs. 11.9 A & B). The Marathon isn't a race, it's a pace, and you need to come in within your time allowed, with a three-minute window if you arrive early. A Training Level VSE needs to travel at 9km/hour to come in at the correct time.

A

B

At some point prior to the start of the Marathon, there will be a course walk so that you know where it goes—and you will receive a map. The course is clearly marked, with numerical gates that you must pass through to stay on course, as well as kilometer markers so you can monitor your time and see if you need to adjust your speed to stay within the time allowed.

The Marathon obstacles won't be included in the course walk, but you are welcome to walk them on your own as many times as you'd like prior to the start of the first horse on course. Each Marathon obstacle, which you may often hear referred to as a "hazard," consists of a series of gates, marked with letters. These must be negotiated in order, with red on right. At Training Level you only have to complete A, B, and C, and your time in the hazard doesn't count. At Preliminary and above, you get penalty points for every second you are in each hazard, so you need to negotiate them as quickly and efficiently, as possible. You use more of the gates as you move up the levels. Missing a gate or negotiating one backward without correcting your mistake results in elimination.

11.9 A & B John Lobo and Cajonat's Orion make time through the water hazard (A). At Training level, there is always a path to negotiate the gates without needing to go into the water, but at upper levels there may be a gate (as marked by the red and white letters) right in the water. Once you move out of Training level, you rack up penalty points for every second it takes you to complete each marathon obstacle. So you need to be very fast and very accurate—this is when it really gets to be fun (B)!

At the upper levels, competitors often have a different carriage for Marathon versus Dressage and Cones, but at Training Level, whatever safe, sturdy vehicle you usually use is acceptable. Pneumatic (air-filled), wire-spoked tires are allowed at Training Level only, at the discretion of the show management, and as most Miniature Horse carts come with pneumatic tires, you'll need to switch them out for solid metal or wooden wheels before moving up to Preliminary.

Depending on the rules of the governing body overseeing the event, you may be required to carry a spares kit. The items required will be outlined in the entry information, but generally, you need things that will help you should you have an equipment failure. A halter and lead for each horse in your turnout, a rein or rein splice, and trace or trace splice, a leather punch, and more. There will again be a safety check prior to the start of Marathon, and you will need to show your spares kit.

You need a stopwatch to monitor your time on Marathon, and some way to keep your paperwork under control. You may want to carry your course maps, a chart showing what your optimal time at each kilometer marker, and you'll always need a space to put your green card, given to you at the start line and handed in at the finish.

Everyone on your carriage must wear a helmet, and a chest protector (flak jacket) is sometimes required for any juniors participating. When you are competing a single VSE, you don't need a groom or navigator, but if you are driving a pair, a tandem, or a four-in-hand, you need a second person with you.

The Marathon is lots of fun for both you and your horse, but only if you are properly prepared. The good news is that Miniature Horses tend to gain fitness very quickly, so if you put the time in, they should easily be able to handle the challenge. If you haven't been able to spend time conditioning your horse in the weeks or months leading up to the competition, it won't be fair to your horse to ask him to do something he isn't physically prepared for. If you are worried that your horse might not be ready to compete in the Marathon, you may be able to only enter the Dressage and Cones sections, or you can do the Marathon but very carefully monitor your horse as you go along to make sure you're not overdoing it. You are able to withdraw at any time if you feel you've reached the limits of your horse's fitness.

At full CDE's you will drive first over distance at a trot, then a walk section, following which there is a vet check. You have a time limit during which you can cool your horse with water and help him get his vital signs back to normal so that the vet will okay him to move on to the final section of the Marathon, where you will find the marathon obstacles. At the end, a second vet check confirms that your horse came through in acceptable condition.

The Marathon can seem very confusing at first. There are a lot of elements to it, and probably the best way to learn is just to spend some time at events as a volunteer. Often at smaller events, someone may need a navigator and you can learn the ropes as a passenger first. Everything is very well marked, however, and usually, once you've done a course walk and spent some time plotting your path through the hazards, you'll do fine once you get out on course. Just always remember: Red on Right.

As with Dressage, your Marathon start time will be posted ahead of time so you are able to plan accordingly. A warm-up for Marathon shouldn't be too extensive as you want to warm the muscles up to avoid injury but not use up the horse's energy and make him tired. You'll need to allow time for your safety check, and be near the start gate in lots of time. Check in with the

"I bought my first Miniature Horse to drive after my friend had a carriage-driving accident and I helped her find a pony to gain her confidence back. I loved hers so much I had to have one of my own."

Hilda Wilkins, Royal Mule Acres

11.10 The clearance on each set of cones is adjusted for each driver depending on the carriage and level of competition. Penalties are assessed for knocking down a ball or going over the time allowed.

starter so she knows you are nearby and ready to go, and she will give you your green card. As your time gets close, the starter will update you on how much time you have, warning you as your time gets close, and then a 10-second countdown before telling you to have a good time. You can't cross the start line prior to your time, but you don't have to start from a standstill.

At the finish of each section, you need to show the green card given to you by the starter so it can updated with your times as you move along, and hand it in at the end of the Marathon so your final score can be calculated.

"Back in the 1990s and early 2000s, I did breed shows, preferring performance events and the 'all-around' horse. I've had my fill of that, though, and now just enjoy driving Miniature Horses for my own pleasure, and simply having them around as company."

Margo Cox-Townsend, Jess Miniature Horses

Cones

In a full CDE, Cones takes place on the third day, after Marathon (fig. 11.10). It is intended to demonstrate your horse's ability to still be fast and accurate after the athletic feat of the Marathon the day before.

Twenty sets of cones, each with a ball on top, must be negotiated within the time limit for your level. Each set of cones is numbered and marked, once again with red on the right, and the course must be navigated in order; going off course will result in elimination. Penalty points are assessed each time a ball is knocked from a cone, and for going over the time limit.

Unlike in Marathon, where you can use a different vehicle and harness, for Cones you must use the same equipment that you did for Dressage. Your dress should also be in the style of Dressage. You get a map of the cones course, and you can walk it as many times as you like prior to the start of that portion of the competition. While the course is numbered, and you can see the next number from the previous pair of cones, if you're not clear on which way to look, it can be very easy to get lost and lose precious seconds searching for the next number.

At a full CDE, once again your start time will be posted. At a driving trial, often your Cones time will be immediately following your Dressage test. Your wheel width will be measured at some point prior to the start of Cones, likely during your first safety check, and each set of cones will be adjusted prior to your start time according the amount of clearance given for your level and turn-out. This number will be in the entry information, so you will know what to expect.

Accuracy is more important than speed, as time penalties add up less quickly than knocked-down balls.

Scoring

At the end of a Combined Driving competition, all your penalty points are added up from the three phases, and the lowest score or least penalty points is the winner. Classes are placed individually (Training Single VSE, for example) and over-all for each level. You get detailed score sheets so you can see where your strengths and weaknesses lie, and know what to work on for next time. One of the great appeals of Combined Driving is that you are first competing against yourself, always striving to improve the performance of yourself and your horse.

Combined Driving is a great way to both have fun with your driving horse, and to advance and refine the skills of both yourself and your horse. This sort of driving appeals to a broad range of drivers—from those who simply enjoy a fun day of driving with friends, to others who enjoy the competitive aspect and constantly challenging themselves.

Pleasure Shows

Pleasure Driving Shows are the showcase of the history and tradition of carriage driving. This is a chance to show off your formal equipment, grooming skills, and best driving hat, as well as your skills and performance. As with Combined Driving, Pleasure Shows are a lovely chance to drive with a diverse group of equines, without the pressure of the fitness requirements.

Equipment

Pleasure Driving Shows are formal events. While you're certainly welcome to attend with a simple metal, easy-entry cart, this is a showcase for more formal vehicles, and your placings, particularly in the Turnout class, will reflect more casual equipment (fig. 11.11). If you have options available, it is more appropriate to choose a leather harness than betathane. Dress yourself as you would for a Dressage test, and pay attention to all those little turnout tips and tricks that you can find on traditional driving.

11.11 A Pleasure Driving show is a formal occasion, rooted in the tradition of carriage driving.

Classes

There are a variety of classes included in a Pleasure Driving show, and while there is some variation on some of the fun classes included, the standard classes are usually the ones included for high point awards.

11.12 Enchanted Acres Rising Sun and Lyle Dietz with their first place ribbon in Working.

11.13 Kathleen Winfield and her pair show in Cross-Country Fault Obstacle at Spruce Meadows Festival of Carriages.

Working

Working is the class where you showcase the talent of your horse (fig. 11.12). Your class will be judged all together, and usually the VSEs and Small Ponies are split from the larger ponies and horses. The gaits required are slow trot, working trot, strong trot, and walk, and the horses need to stand quietly in line and rein back at the direction of the judge.

Reinsmanship

In Reinsmanship, the driver's ability is rewarded. Turnouts are worked both directions of the arena, and then will be asked to perform individually to allow the judge to evaluate the skill of the drivers in handling their horse.

Turnout

Turnout is judged both on the attractiveness of the whole entry, and also the appropriateness and suitability. The class is run as with Working, with the same gaits and ring procedure.

Cross-Country Fault Obstacle

Similar to a Cones course, horses must negotiate a series of gates around a number of natural obstacles without going off course or knocking any cones (fig. 11.13). It is a timed competition with both accuracy and efficiency included in the scoring of the event.

Other Classes

There is a wide variety of other classes that can be included in a Pleasure Show, and described prize list, as well as information about which classes you need to enter to qualify for high point awards.

Chapter 12:
More Miniature Horse Activities

"But What Can You Do with a Miniature Horse?"

If you have ever expressed your interest in Miniature Horses to others, chances are you've heard this question. Even beyond the obvious choices of showing, driving, and breeding (see p. 158), people have fun with their Miniatures in so many ways, and these are just a few you might want to explore.

Horse Agility

Horse Agility is a relatively new activity, and one that more people are discovering every day. Any horse can do Horse Agility, and the organization overseeing the sport (the International Horse Agility Club—www.thehorseagilityclub.com) is set up with increasing levels so that you and your horse develop your skills gradually and set you up for success.

What Is It?
A series of obstacles are negotiated, either on a lead or at liberty, with a strong emphasis on good horsemanship and working with your horse rather than controlling him through force (figs. 12.1 A & B). You may be asked to negotiate a pattern around cones, work over poles or tarps, or walk your horse under a curtain or through a tunnel. Obstacles are

12.1 A & B Circle J Sir John Eh (Johnnie) walks through the water bottles while practicing for his Horse Agility pattern at liberty (A), then he walks through the curtain (B).

Miniature Tales
Rocky

Rocky was a bit of a challenging young stallion. He was good natured and generally very well behaved, but his short attention span and lack of focus meant that his training needed to be approached a lot more slowly. Horse Agility seemed like a perfect winter activity for the two of us, both because it could be done in the snow, or tucked into the barn, and because it would be an incentive to get me out there and work with him on a regular basis even in the cold and dark winter months.

Agility was not only great fun, but the emphasis on a loose lead and allowing the horse to negotiate each obstacle was a bit of an epiphany for both of us. As a long-time exhibitor of Miniature Horses, I had that competitive perfectionism, and it improved my horsemanship greatly to have to allow Rocky to negotiate each obstacle without my directing his every step. For him, being given that responsibility, made a huge different in his focus. Now he had to use his brain and problem-solve what was required, as I wasn't going to do his thinking for him.

Each month as I had the course set up to enter Rocky's pattern, I also used it for other horses, especially my two yearlings that would play through the obstacles at liberty, having a lot of fun and good experiences. While other things keep me busy in the summer, Agility has become a fun and very beneficial winter activity at our barn.

usually simple to build, and are a great tool to create a trusting relationship with your horse. Agility courses are scored on completion of each obstacle in the pattern, and points are deducted for each mistake, including such things as hitting a pole rather than stepping over it, mistakes on the pattern, or a tightening of the lead rope, showing a lack of teamwork.

While practicing agility courses can be a fun and productive way to spend time with your horse, a competition is a good way to get an impartial evaluation of how your training has improved. If you wish to participate in the online competition, you download the current course for your level, build the obstacles, practice with your horse, and then have someone video you and your horse completing the course as instructed. You send your entry in, and will get not only a score and points towards moving up to the next level, but also comments on where points were lost and what was done well. A new course is posted each month for a new competition. There are even ribbons and prizes that are mailed out to you following each class, and a high point competition each year.

More traditional, live competitions are also available in some areas, but the ability to train and compete without having to leave your home barn is a popular advantage.

"Just spending time with Miniatures, sitting down with them and visiting…working them is great, but just 'horse time' is the best."

Joan McNaughton

Because it isn't a ridden sport, Miniature Horses are well suited for agility work.

Benefits

Just like Halter Obstacle (see p. 121) in the breed shows for Miniature Horses, negotiating obstacles is a very good challenge. Working on Agility skills develops the horse/human partnership, as well as improving the horse's ground manners and maneuverability.

In Horse Agility you are penalized each time your lead rope becomes tight, so there is a strong focus on allowing your horse to complete the challenge in front of him without force or you controlling his every move. Since Miniature Horses are all too often—usually inadvertently, but not always—manhandled into doing what is asked of them, this rule allows them to be more of an active participant in the process, rather than simply doing as directed because they have no other choice.

Trick Training

Love spending time with your horse in a fun activity that will make your bond stronger and give you some adorable skills to show off to your friends? Then trick training might be for you (fig. 12.2)!

It's easy for some to dismiss trick training as a foolish pursuit, but not only does it engage your horse's brain by asking him to problem-solve what behavior you are looking for, but it strengthens your bond and improves your ability to work as a team with your horse. Trick training can be the bridge you need to get through to a difficult horse, or the tactic you can use to teach a very useful skill—being caught, for instance, or trailer loading. Not to mention that it is lots of fun to show off the results of your playtime with your

12.2 Circle J Hawk shows off his rear on command.

Miniature Horse, demonstrating his new tricks for your friends!

Positive Reinforcement

Because tricks are usually taught using positive reinforcement such as a food reward, horses tend to be very motivated to continue to offer learned behaviors, and keen to practice new ones. Most traditional horse training is done with negative reinforcement, which means that something (generally, pressure when referring to horse training) is *taken away* to tell the horse that he has the right answer. For example, you want him to move away from you: you tap on his shoulder and cluck until he steps away—then you stop tapping his shoulder. Positive reinforcement means something is *added*, that is, as soon as the horse gives the response you are looking for, he is rewarded, usually with

12.3 A useful trick: Johnnie was very difficult to load into a trailer, but through learning to follow a target (the rainbow crop) he quickly learned to load with enthusiasm.

a treat. As a food reward is a primary reinforcement for a horse, it is very powerful and gives him a much more positive feeling about the behavior than one trained by using negative reinforcement.

By pairing your positive reinforcement with a "bridge" signal such as a verbal cue ("Good!") or a clicker, you can use all the good feelings created by the food reward in other situations as well. Maybe you used this method to teach your horse to pick up a toy and bring it to you because it was fun for both of you. But now, when you are working on your extended trot in harness and your horse gives you exactly what you're looking for, you can use that verbal reinforcement that he now understands because of his trick training, and say "Good!" and he will get the same

positive feeling that he gets when he receives a food reward (fig. 12.3).

The science of positive reinforcement is very interesting, and hugely beneficial in training Miniature Horses. Trick training is a great way to start exploring it for your horses.

Parades

It can be great fun to show your Miniature Horse off in your local parade. Whether they are working in harness, or being led in hand wearing the colors of the current celebration, Miniature Horses are always a hit and will be enjoyed by everyone in your community.

Preparation

Preparing your horse for a parade goes far beyond brushing and decorating. A parade is one of the more challenging experiences for a horse to deal with, as he can run into things at a parade he might never encounter anywhere else. From enthusiastic crowds of people, to floats, marching bands, and stray balloons, there are many things to startle a flight animal. Do what you can to expose him to parade-type experiences beforehand, but more importantly, teach him how to safely react to new things. You are never going to be able to introduce him to everything he could possibly encounter, but you can show him that you can be trusted to keep him safe. This way, when you suddenly find yourself in the parade order behind the whip cracker or the quick-draw artist, you'll be able to still have a safe and fun parade.

In the interest of safety, it's a good idea to have extra walkers with you. In many parades, a header to walk along with each horse is required. Especially when you are driving your horses in the parade, having extra hands on the ground

Miniature Tales
Hawk

While most Miniature Horses love to be a part of whatever you are doing, Hawk didn't like anything to do with people. Leading, brushing, and hoof care were always a big deal as we struggled to convince him that we really were on his side. As he matured, he improved and became a good driving horse, but while he did what was asked of him, he never really seemed to be engaged.

Then I taught him some tricks. His first trick was rearing, which is absolutely not the first trick you should teach to any horse, let alone a challenging one, but it was a behavior that Hawk offered on his own, standing on his hind legs in his stall and banging the gate with his front feet to let you know it was time for his breakfast. Immediately, I noticed a difference in his enthusiasm for all his training, and started teaching him more tricks. He learned to nod and shake his head on command, started to learn to Spanish Walk, and more importantly, he engaged with me for the first time in his life as we played these new games together. Even driving became more fun, as it felt more like play as well, and he had more and more success as a combined driving horse.

It wasn't until after his driving career was cut short by injury that Hawk really found his calling. I taught him to paint, and painting is what Hawk loves most in the world (fig. 12.4). He quickly realized that he was able to make a mark on the paper, and then explored applying the paint to

12.4 *Hawk's very favorite trick is painting.*

other things: the ground, the fence, me, and the barn cat, for example.

The proof that painting is Hawk's favorite thing in the world? Hawk was nearly impossible to catch his entire life in anything but the smallest pen. Even when he was driving competitively and seemed to enjoy it, I still had no chance of catching him at pasture without bringing him into a smaller pen first. But after he learned to paint? All I have to do is call and he will come. He hasn't painted in the better part of a year right now, but he is still easy to catch, and sometimes hard to get rid of as he will block my path, attempting to offer every trick he knows in the hopes of a cookie or some attention.

Trick training truly brought out Hawk's personality in a way nothing else I had tried could do. The improved confidence and engagement it gave him benefited everything I did with him, and I now do a little trick training with almost all the horses that I work with, especially the challenging or nervous ones.

12.5 *My Grandparents, Merv and Claudia Giles, really enjoyed traveling to parades with their eight-horse hitch of black Miniature geldings.*

*Equine Assisted Learning and
Equine Assisted Therapy*

Using horses as a part of psychotherapy, or to teach life skills, is a rapidly growing modality (figs. 12.6 A & B). Julia Morgan, of Horse Powered Connections, is a certified FEEL practitioner. FEEL stands for Facilitated Equine Experiential Learning, and horses are a very active participant in the process. Using a horse-led series of exercises, equine experiential learning works with the horse's natural sensitivity to physical movement and emotional states to help people gain self-knowledge and acquire skills leading to personal growth through positive life changes.

Julia's focus is on children. Her journey began with her own son, who was non-verbal and diagnosed as severely autistic. He is now an outgoing, talkative, and confident little boy, a

is a very good idea, even if your horses are very unlikely to have a dramatic reaction. Just because you are confident in your horses, doesn't mean that there won't be a toddler who outruns parents at just the wrong moment, and having someone between the crowd and your horse keeps everyone safe from harm (fig. 12.5).

Therapy Work

The benefits of interaction with horses are only just beginning to be properly explored, and with their unique small size and very curious personality, Miniature Horses are very well suited to be therapy animals.

12.6 A & B Ethan makes a heart connection with Jerome before they begin working together (A). He also syncs his breathing with Jerome—and Jerome with Ethan (B).

transformation that Julia credits to the horses and learning to connect with his environment more like a horse would.

Julia enjoys working with children and finds a special joy in helping children face the challenges arising from ADD (attention deficit disorders), anxiety, and ASD (autism spectrum disorder). She has seen remarkable changes from children's interactions with the horses, from a teenage girl with ADHD (attention deficit hyperactivity disorder) who proclaimed that her brain had never been so quiet, to a young autistic boy who was once again excited to go to school and make new friends because he'd been able to make friends with the horse.

Emotional intelligence, management, nonverbal communication, and connection is a big part of what Julia does for people of all ages, and her clients find great value in the honest, judgment-free responses of the horses. She also works with business and corporate clients, allowing the horses to be the expert instructors in verbal and non-verbal communication, and awareness of the energy they bring to their business interactions, skills that align well with creating good business relationships.

Many of the horses that Julia works with in her program are rescues, some with physical or emotional issues that have benefited dramatically from being a part of a system that listens as carefully to the needs of the horse as it does the human participants. Since Julia's focus is on children, a Miniature Horse seemed like a good addition to the herd.

The small size of the Miniature Horse is ideal for children who might feel intimidated by a full-sized horse, and though Jerome is new to the program, as well as new to working with children, Julia finds him highly intuitive and very concerned

"It's very hard to pick just one thing I like to do with my Miniatures! One: Share your Miniature Horse with others, especially special needs children and adults. Two: We had a 4-H club for several years and used our horses as 4-H projects for the members. They learned how to train them to drive from harnessing and ground driving, to then introducing them to the cart. Sledding with the Miniature Horses was part of the training and probably everyone's favorite thing to do with them. Three: I recommend online horse agility, from training and improving communication with your horse to entering online competitions against others doing the same thing from all over the world (and with different size equines)."

Mary Adams, On Target Miniatures

about the well-being of his small charges. Jerome has some soundness issues that preclude him from a career as a performance horse, but he is keen to work at his new job, one that is low impact but mentally stimulating.

Pet Therapy and Visitations

The idea that spending time with horses is therapeutic isn't a new one. The oft-used quote, "The outside of a horse is good for the inside of a man," has been around so long that we aren't even sure who said it. But far beyond anecdote, studies have shown that horses do have therapeutic value in many ways (fig. 12.7).

Miniature Horses are uniquely suited to many aspects of pet therapy, with their small size allowing them access to places that regular horses simply couldn't go. The temperament of a Miniature

12.7 *Residents and guests alike enjoy the Miniature Horses in the beautiful courtyard at Kensington.*

12.8 *Feeding carrots and other goodies to the Miniature Horses is a favorite pasttime of residents—and the horses!*

is smart and curious, and like all horses, they are highly intuitive, seeming to just "know" when they need to be extra gentle with those around them.

At the Shepard's Care Kensington Campus, in Edmonton, Alberta, Miniature Horses are involved in a unique program. As an "aging in place" facility, Kensington is home to 600 residents, and offers every form of housing, from independent

apartments to assisted living and long-term care. The beautiful and spacious courtyard at the center of the facility is home to fountains, trees, flowers, and vegetable gardens, and the winding pathways take you to a small barn and paddock where residents can visit Miniature Horses.

The vision and dedication of Dan Bisson, Recreation Manager at Kensington, was the driving force behind this unique program first established in 2010. Throughout the summer months, two Miniature Horses live on campus for two-week intervals, and Dan says there have been three major benefits for the residents of Kensington (fig. 12.8).

First, it gets more people outside and into the courtyard. The day I visited, as soon as the horses arrived for another two-week stay, residents—who must have been watching from windows awaiting the horses' arrival—appeared with bags of carrots (fig. 12.9). Several residents told me they come every day to see the horses, another that he checks on them every night before bed.

The second benefit that quickly became

12.9 *Peter and Terry Holt with Dan Bisson in front of the barn and paddock where the horses live when on site at Kensington.*

obvious was that the residents received more visitors during the times that the horses were on site, and they were able to share the enjoyment with their children and grandchildren. And the third benefit that Dan outlined was they were able take the horses inside the building to visit residents who aren't mobile, giving everyone the opportunity to enjoy and interact with the horses, an activity that wouldn't be possible with a regular-sized horse. Residents who can't go outside enjoy watching them from their window, and many make a point of checking on them regularly.

The horses involved in this exceptional program usually live at Hollyhock Meadow, a Miniature Horse farm not far from the city, with owners Peter and Terry Holt. Peter and Terry are dedicated to sharing their horses with others, and spend their summers with a steady stream of pet-therapy commitments, both taking their horses to visit others, and having groups tour the farm (figs. 12.10 A & B).

The groups are mostly from seniors' care homes, but they also work with people with Down syndrome and special needs children. There are endless stories about reactions from people who haven't responded to anything in years, ranging from the big smile from petting a horse, to a child that is never still, sitting quietly and enjoying a ride in a cart behind a calm and experienced Miniature Horse.

Visits usually involve not only petting and interacting with the horses, but watching them drive and jump, a ride on the "wedding wagon" behind The Governor and The General, and a hot dog roasted over a fire in the fresh air. Terry says they can reach more people by taking the horses to the facility, but the quality of the experience is better when the people come to them, and sometimes it's just the smell of the campfire that brings the biggest smile of the day (fig. 12.11). The dedication of the care staff has a lot to do with how well such visits go. Many members of the staff will do everything they can to get residents onto a cart for a ride if that's what they want, and that makes such a difference in the experience.

12.10 A & B Duane Kary and Paddy sharing the joy (A) and Peter Holt and Cheerio give cart rides (B).

12.11 *Hollyhock Meadow The Governor and Hollyhock Meadow The General take visitors for a ride in the "Wedding Wagon" through the pastures at Hollyhock Meadow.*

12.12 *First Knights Special Bit O Rowdy shows off his jumping skills for visitors.*

"I love driving, and Combined Driving is our favorite sport. I also love sharing my passion for true horsemanship with my kids, and the Miniatures have provided my kids with the confidence to 'play' with horses without the intimidation of size."

Tamara Chmilar

If your interest is in pet therapy and sharing your horses with others, you'll need a horse that shares it. Based on Peter and Terry's experience, horses that are too quiet don't make the best choice because they are less likely to engage and interact with people. A horse with a natural curiosity that is bold and brave enough to enjoy new things and going to new places is ideal (fig. 12.12).

While these have been very specific examples of Miniature Horses being used for a therapeutic purpose, there are so many ways that you can share your horses to make people smile, and lots of organizations that can help you along the way (fig. 12.13).

Riding

In general, Miniature Horses are not well suited to be saddle horses. Small children can certainly sit on them, and they can be excellent lead-line mounts, but often, by the time children are big enough to actually be able to start riding on their own, they are beginning to outgrow a Miniature (fig. 12.14).

The universal guideline for how much a horse can carry, including rider and tack, is 20 percent of his body weight. With an average 250-pound, 34-inch Miniature Horse, this means a child should be no more than 50 pounds to sit on him. A larger Miniature Horse, at 350 pounds, could carry children up to 70 pounds, and might be able to be a proper first mount.

In no case should Miniatures ever be ridden by an adult, not even for a second for a funny photo. They simply are not built to carry a full-size person, and the strain could cause serious injury. This can be a problem for training purposes; when an adult cannot ride and train them, it is going to

12.13 Thumbelina, a dwarf, visits with visitors. An experienced therapy horse, she is very comfortable with wheelchairs and other equipment.

12.14 While many good natured Miniature Horses can become comfortable with small children sitting on them for a short ride, more serious riding will require correct training and careful monitoring.

be tricky to create a horse that will be safe and responsive for a young rider.

Like all ponies and horses, it is unfair to both the horse and the child to simply turn them loose together and hope for the best. Children don't have the skill and knowledge to train a horse, and inconsistent, unintentionally unfair handling is at the root of most of the "bad pony" stigma.

There are many Miniature Horses, carefully trained and properly supervised, that make exceptional children's mounts, teaching their small charges—under the guidance of an instructor—to be proper young horsemen and horsewomen. But just because a Miniature is the right size for a child to ride does not mean that he is ready for the job, and it would be unreasonable to expect him to behave appropriately without the training to do so.

Some Miniature Horse breeders will not sell a horse to someone who intends to use him for riding. If riding is your goal, you need to get a horse well-suited in size and conformation, as well as properly trained for job you're asking him to do.

For many years, Miniature Horses were bred as draft animals. They are much stronger and better suited for pulling and working as carriage horses, than they are saddle horses.

The Sky Is the Limit

It is great fun to see the wide variety of activities that Miniature Horses can do with their humans. They can succeed in so many activities: from performers in trick and liberty shows, to miniature chuck-wagon or chariot racing; from high-level dressage complete with airs above the ground performed on long lines or at liberty, to pulling a sled or skijoring for winter fun (fig. 12.15).

Miniature Horses are smart, bold, and very keen to learn something new. They love to be a part of whatever you're doing, and the activities you can participate in with your Miniature Horse are limited only by your imagination.

When you have your Miniature Horses out and about, it isn't unusual for people to ask you,

"But what are they good for?" I tell them about their history, how they are descended from the pit ponies, and they say, "So, now they're just pets?" I always find that a little bit of an odd response. All types of horses once had important jobs. Humanity wouldn't have achieved what it has without the horse, and many of the modern breeds we have today are a result of a specific purpose in history. For example, draft horses had to be big and strong to work in the fields, or carry a knight in full armor, or transport heavy freight where it needed to go. Today though, what is any horse "good for"? They are no longer necessary for our survival, but that doesn't mean they are any less valuable. Horses, of all sizes and shapes, enrich our lives in so many ways, and Miniature Horses are no exception.

Even just time spent caring for them can be enjoyable enough that many people do keep them simply as pets. While the daily chores involved in caring for my herd is often the best part of my day, Miniature Horses also love to have a job, so

12.15 Kathleen Winfield and her pair enjoy some winter fun!

exploring activities that you and your horses can enjoy together is time well spent. It doesn't have to be a huge investment of time or money; I teach tricks while feeding them breakfast, and set up simple agility courses right in the pasture that they then rearrange for me while they play with and without supervision. Driving is, in my opinion, the most fun you can have with your Miniature and opens up a whole new world of activities you can participate in. Really, the sky is the limit when it comes to answering that question (figs. 12.16 A & B).

12.16 A & B Circle J On The Rocks poses for a Christmas Card photo—he's an excellent sport considering he is a breeding stallion (A)! Tayten Wagar shows off her excellent "Frozen"- themed costume for the Youth Costume class at a Miniature Horse show (B).

PART 5:

Breeding

Chapter 13:

Is It Right For You?

Breeding Options

Before deciding you are going to raise Miniature Horses, take a long, hard look at the industry as a whole. Horses, in general, are being produced at a rate that isn't sustainable. In parts of the world where horse slaughter has been banned, there is no recourse for those unwanted horses, with no one to spend the money for their proper feeding and care. Horses are dying of neglect and in all sorts of undesirable situations and Miniature Horses are no exception. Because of their small size, many people start breeding them as a novelty, with no regard for the quality of the horses they are raising. Go to nearly any livestock auction and you will find unregistered, untrained, and uncared for Miniature Horses being sold at giveaway prices.

If you are simply raising Miniature Horses because "they are cute," there is a better way for you to have them in your life (fig. 13.1). Go to that same auction and give a good home to a Miniature Horse that needs you. That's the thing about Miniatures—they're small enough that they're still cute as adults. You don't need to have a baby (or eight) each year, just to have the cute factor.

Ask the Hard Questions First

Before you breed your first mare, or purchase a mare in foal, you need to plan for the future. Do you have the knowledge to see that mare and her foal safely through foaling? Are you prepared for a potentially significant vet bill if she needs help? What is your plan for this foal? If you intend to sell him, will he have the registration, conformation, athleticism, temperament, and good foundation of training to make him marketable in your area? Are you prepared to keep the foal for as long as necessary to find the appropriate long-term home, even if that means you keep him forever?

13.1 There isn't much cuter than a miniature foal, but think very hard about whether you're prepared for everything that comes with the cuteness.

And the biggest question of all—are you prepared to potentially lose your mare? It isn't a high probability, but it is a risk taken every time a mare is bred, and even if it isn't a likely outcome, it is one that needs to be taken seriously.

Long-Term Plan

Any foal you bring into this world puts the onus on you to give him every chance for a long, healthy and useful life. That starts with choosing a mare and stallion that will, you hope (breeding is not an exact science, which adds to the risk portion of the equation), produce a foal with the temperament, conformation, and talent for the job you have in mind. If you are producing a foal without a goal in mind, this might be a red flag.

Do you have the skill and knowledge to care for and train that foal so he grows to his potential? If not, do you have the connections and resources to see that he gets the good start he needs in life and in his career?

While it would be great to say that you will ensure that foal has a good life for all of his days, that isn't always in our control. Things happen; even horses we intend to keep always may one day find themselves in a new home. What we can control is making sure that those horses are good citizens with skills and other assets, such as registration, to give them as many options as possible, making them more likely to find one of the precious "good homes."

Facilities

Before you plan for your first foal, you need to know where you're going to foal this mare out. Not only do you need a safe space to contain mare and foal, but a good way to monitor the mare during foaling. Things can go wrong very

13.2 *Foal-safe fencing is an important consideration before deciding to breed your mare.*

quickly, so the sooner you are aware that she's foaling, the better. Mares can absolutely foal outdoors (with protection from the elements, of course) or in a generously sized box stall, but in both situations they need to be checked on frequently, and a camera system allows you do so with the most convenience.

Then it's time to consider where this foal is going to live as he grows. Are your pasture fences appropriate for a foal, so he can safely be turned out with his mother (fig. 13.2)? Do you have separate safe paddocks or pens available so you can wean your foal when the time comes, without mare or foal getting hurt trying to get back together?

Education

Foaling is a dangerous time for both mare and foal, but you can mitigate that risk by educating yourself on what to expect and knowing how to

"Buy the finest quality mares and stallions you can afford. We all have to start somewhere, but you can always find that special horse if you look. Bloodlines are extremely important. Get a good book and read everything you can about breeding your mare and the consequences. Breeding isn't for everyone, nor should it be."

Linda and Peter Spahr, Hanlin Farm

recognize a problem early. I have given a brief overview of what to expect here, but there are excellent books (two I like are *Complete Foaling Manual* by Teresa Jones and *Blessed Are the Broodmares* by M. Phyllis Lose) available to give you an in-depth look at everything foaling. Remember, the more you know, the more you are likely to be able to help your mare when she needs you. Learning about foaling is scary, as it can seem that with so much to go wrong, how are there any healthy, normal foals born at all? The good news is that most foalings are completely normal, but by educating yourself about all the bad things, you'll be able to recognize them and get your mare and foal the help they need.

A good relationship with your vet is critical at this point. Discuss your plan for foaling, make sure the vet is aware when your mare is showing signs that she is close, and decide if you are immediately going to have a veterinarian come out, wait for a 24-hour checkup and IgG (immunoglobulin G/antibody) check, or only call if you have a concern.

Buying Instead of Breeding

Remember, before you embark on this breeding thing, you can absolutely add to your herd without breeding. In fact, purchasing a new horse has many advantages to raising a foal. Breeding is always a gamble, but when you're buying a horse, you can wait until you find the horse with the gender, size, temperament, conformation, and even the training and color you like best.

While it might seem like it's more affordable to breed a mare than it is to buy a mature horse, if you add up the cost of caring for the mare, caring for the foal, feeding and training the foal, potential vet bills, all the years of vaccination, farrier care, and deworming, chances are you'll be saving money by "only" paying the purchase price of the horse. And you'll be getting exactly what you ordered! Seriously consider buying instead of breeding. It's almost always the sensible option.

The Stallion Factor

Owning a Stallion

It is very common in Miniature Horses for everyone who is raising foals to have their own stallion. It's easy to see why—in larger breeds, housing a stallion requires special facilities, and handling one requires special training. Miniature Horse stallions are obviously much smaller and generally good natured, so the simple act of owning one isn't prohibitive. Because of this, there are a lot of stallions that probably don't have the quality to remain a stallion. Just because they're not that much trouble to keep around and they make it easy to have cute foals isn't enough of a reason to keep a stallion.

But if you have one you feel has the conformation, temperament, talent, and training to pass on his genes to your future foals, you'll likely have good luck with breeding your mares to your own stallion.

Breeding to an Outside Stallion

In most of the horse industry, because of the difficulty in keeping and handling a stallion, breeders choose to breed their mares to outside stallions. In addition to having the advantage of not having to keep a stallion of your own—because let's face it, even tiny stallions can be noisy pains in the management system—you can choose the stallion that best complements each mare, rather than using one stallion for all your mares. It gives you a much wider genetic base to draw upon (fig. 13.3).

When breeding to a stallion that stands to the public, you pay a "stud fee," take your mare to the stallion's farm, he does his thing, and you pick her up a few weeks later and expect your foal in about 11 months. Mares don't always play by the rules, however, so things might not go quite that smoothly. Most stallion owners offer some sort of a breed-back option. For instance, when your mare doesn't catch, you can breed again the following year (perhaps for a nominal "chute fee"—a portion of the stud fee), or if your mare loses her foal and there is a "live foal guarantee" as part of your breeding contract, you can rebreed the following year on the same stud fee.

Be sure to get a contract from the stallion owner and clarify these details, as well as any mare-care fees (board charges to cover her feed and care while she is at the breeding farm) and

13.3 Breeding your mare to an outside stallion gives you more options and fewer management issues than owning a stallion of your own.

consider insurance on her while she is out of your control. They are horses, after all, and horses do love to find a way to injure themselves.

AI/Shipped/Frozen Semen

Another option to look at is breeding your mare via artificial insemination with cooled shipped semen. This allows you the unique opportunity to breed to a stallion that isn't in your local area. Your veterinarian will need to monitor your mare for

"First, ask yourself why are you thinking about breeding? Does it make sense? Are the mare and stallion both good quality and healthy animals? What are you going to do with the foal? Will the offspring be an improvement over the mare/stallion? What attributes are you trying to breed for? Just because they are little doesn't mean every horse should be bred."

Pip Breckon

"When breeding, conformation is #1, temperament #2, pedigree #3, color is always last. If you are lucky to find all of this, you are good to go."

Melissa Cooney, Fuller Creek Miniatures

impending ovulation. At the right time, they order a shipment of semen from the stallion you've chosen, and it is sent overnight via courier or airline, and inseminated into your mare near the time of her ovulation.

There are a few Miniature Horse stallions offering shipped cooled semen as a breeding option, though frozen semen (which allows more convenient shipping, but slightly lower conception rates) is not commonplace and isn't permitted for registration at this time.

While this can be an exciting way to bring a popular bloodline into your herd, the costs involved can be quite significant, both for monitoring and breeding of the mare, as well as semen shipment. The conception rates, while quite respectable, are not nearly as good as mares bred via live cover. Be sure to look into all the costs involved, and decide up front how many cycles you are going to try so you don't get into too much money with no pregnancy. Remember that even a healthy pregnancy is no guarantee of a healthy foal.

Stallion Handling

As mentioned, due to the small size and general good nature of Miniature stallions, many people have their own. It is important to remember that just because they are small it doesn't mean they should be forgiven for misbehaving. Stallions need to be held to the same standards of behavior as you would expect from a mare or a gelding; the only exception is during breeding, and even then they must be respectful of their handler (fig. 13.4). If you wouldn't let your mare drag you around or display dangerous behavior such as biting or striking, don't allow it from your stallion. "Because he's a stallion," is not an excuse.

Be the Alpha Mare

Stallions may act as if they want to be the boss, but they're wrong. Being the one in charge stresses them out. Often, when a stallion has gained a reputation for being "dangerous," it's simply that he believes he's in charge of his human and doesn't know how to deal with that kind of responsibility. In a herd situation, the stallion watches for danger and keeps his herd together, but it's the alpha mare who is the boss. She says, "Jump," and he says, "How high?" Be the alpha mare.

13.4 Stallions will test your fencing much more than mares and geldings. You definitely need to keep them safe and secure.

Good Discipline

You can learn from the boss mare. When the stallion steps out of line, what does she do? Chances are, she squeals bloody murder and boots him in the ribs as many times as she can before he wises up and answers with, "Ma'am, yes ma'am." It's the squealing part that's key with a stallion. So when he does the same to you, yell at him—really holler. Make yourself big, get in his space, and make him back away from you. As soon as you've made your point—and do it fast, because after only a few seconds he'll have forgotten what you're so mad about—then go back to business as usual until the next time he steps out of line.

When a Stallion Needs to Act Like a Stallion

You are going to need to let a stallion act like a stallion in order to breed your mares. (If you aren't planning to use your stallion for breeding, he should be gelded, but that's a discussion for another time.) Stallions aren't stupid; they can learn that there is a time and a place for breeding behavior. Just like any sort of horse training, in the beginning, you need to make it very clear to them what you expect. Be consistent. Always breed in the same place—in the stallion's own paddock is a good idea, then, any time he leaves his space, he is expected to behave. If that's not an option, just be sure that all the breeding is done in the same spot. Use a specific halter, only for breeding, possibly with a chain over his nose. A chain can be used both as a cue that this is breeding time and for additional control if needed.

Down to Business

Tease the stallion—allow him to safely interact with the mare—until he's ready to breed. If you're a beginner at handling one, tease through a fence first; it will be just as effective but you'll have more control over the situation. Never let the stallion mount before he's ready to breed—that is, he is fully erect. Allow him to approach the mare from the side, so his shoulder is against her hip. Letting him mount from behind is a good way to get him kicked in his important parts. When he mounts from the side, he'll knock her hip as he goes up, and she'll be too busy getting her balance to let fly with an ill-timed kick. If you watch a stallion in a pasture-breeding situation, this is how he'll mount. When he dismounts, immediately spin the mare's hindquarters away from him, again to prevent an opportunity to kick.

Showing Off

The first time a stallion attends a show or competition, all the strange horses around might just blow his little mind. The same rules apply as to your regular handling and breeding practices: be consistent. And remember, even him simply "screaming" like a stallion is disrespectful because he is not paying attention to you. Get his focus back on you, and give him lots of praise when he makes an effort. If you can, try to get him off the farm a few times before his first show. Take him to a friend's place and work with him in sight of strange horses. Get someone to bring out another stallion and line them up together like in a Halter class. Set your stallion up for success (fig. 13.5).

"Temperament counts, above all. Without a sound mind you have nothing."

Sheila Cook, Double C Miniatures

13.5 *Stallions are very capable of knowing when stallion behavior is appropriate, and when it isn't. In a non-breeding situation, they should be held to the same standards of behavior as any other horse. Circle J On The Rocks, a six-year-old breeding stallion, participates in his first driving clinic.*

13.6 *Your mares should be in good health before breeding, and carry a healthy weight. Overweight mares are more difficult to get in foal.*

A pushy, difficult-to-handle stallion is a struggle to deal with every day. But with consistent handling and clear expectations, a stallion can be just as pleasant and reliable a partner as a mare or a gelding.

Broodmare Care

Average gestation for a horse is 340 days, with normal being from 320 to 360 days. This range is even broader with a Miniature Horse, with normal term foals being born healthy at anywhere from 300 to 370 days gestation. In general, Miniature Horses tend to the lower end of the scale, and most breeders calculate gestation to 320 days for an estimated due date, but watch very closely from 300 days on. It isn't unheard of for Miniature mares to foal normal healthy foals even in the late 290s. Basically, if you have a mare in foal and near the final months of her gestation, you need to be monitoring her closely. Yes, this might mean you start watching her at day 300 and she doesn't foal until day 370, a span of over two months. Did you think this was going to be easy?

Getting in Foal

Before you worry about when to expect that much-anticipated foal, though, you have to first get your mare pregnant, which should be straightforward, but often isn't.

Health and Body Condition

One of the first things you can do is evaluate the health and body condition of your potential broodmare (fig. 13.6). Is she in good physical shape with no health concerns? It is not uncommon for the decision to be made to breed a mare based on her lack of soundness for other activities, but it's important to ensure the unsoundness won't become a welfare concern during pregnancy. Also be very sure that the reason for the unsoundness isn't a predisposition that she is going to pass on to the next generation.

Mares are most fertile when they are in a position to be gaining weight during breeding season. If your mare is too fat or too thin, her fertility can be compromised.

It is a good idea to do a pre-breeding exam with your veterinarian, especially when you are planning to do the higher cost of shipped semen, or even any breeding to an outside stallion. Your veterinarian will check that your mare has no unusual fluid in her uterus, no damage evident from previous foalings, evaluate her risk of infections due to her perineal conformation, and if desired, additional diagnostics such as a culture and biopsy of her uterus to help evaluate her chances of conceiving. Sometimes, this examination will allow you and your vet to make a plan that will help give your mare the very best chance of catching and carrying a foal for you.

Following the Cycle

Mares are in estrus ("in heat" or "in season") every 21 days. While the number of days a mare will show estrus varies, five to seven days is average. Exposing the mare safely, through a fence, to a stallion or sometimes a gelding, allows her to show the signs of estrus and lets you track her cycle effectively (fig. 13.7). When a mare is in estrus, she will display such behavior as urination and posturing, and she usually won't want to leave the stallion. When in diestrus, or not in heat, she will be quite the opposite:

expect squealing, kicking, and attempting to run away as she explains, in no uncertain terms, that she is not interested.

If you are planning to breed at a certain time, it doesn't hurt to track the cycles leading up to the one you intend to breed on as this will allow you to know how long her cycles usually are and, in general, know when to be ready to breed her.

When to Breed

Mares ovulate at the end of the cycle. It's the presence of a large follicle that creates the change in hormones to make her receptive to the stallion, so once that follicle has ovulated, her signs of estrus will subside. As this is the case, it isn't necessary to breed her right at the beginning of the cycle, and you can usually safely wait a couple days before her first breeding. Now, if you've tracked her last two cycles, and they were only three days long, perhaps you'll want to disregard this advice and breed at the first sign of heat. Mares do like to keep you on your toes and they are not good at following rules.

13.7 Qatiana shows signs of estrus to two-year-old stallion Frankie on the other side of the fence.

"Don't breed unless you are experienced, knowledgeable about what is 'correct' in temperament and conformation, and you are prepared to provide the resulting offspring a home for life if necessary."

Margo Cox-Townsend, Jess Miniature Horses

The sperm from the stallion will survive in the reproductive tract of the mare for at least 48 hours. Why is this an important statistic? Because it means that you only need to breed your mare every two days throughout her cycle to keep viable sperm available for when she ovulates. There have been studies done on pasture breeding and wild stallions, and they follow this same pattern: mares are not bred at the very start of estrus, and are only bred every 48 hours or so until they go out of estrus. More frequent breeding will not increase your chances of conception, and may actually be a hindrance as additional fluid in the uterus can cause problems.

Remember to calculate when the foal is likely to arrive prior to breeding—you don't want to suddenly find out that your mare is going to foal in February and you don't have a suitable barn to keep a newborn warm.

Confirming Pregnancy

Once your mare goes out of estrus, it's time to wait and see. There are a couple different approaches you can take. First, and most reliable, is to have your veterinarian ultrasound your mare 16 days after her last breeding date. At this point, the ultrasound will see the vesicle of the new pregnancy,

if, as you are hoping, there is one to be seen. In addition, an ultrasound at this stage can identify a twin pregnancy. While twins are quite rare in horses, and more so in Miniatures, they are not unheard of and can be quite dangerous for the mare and her foals. For this reason, when a twin pregnancy is identified, one of the vesicles is reduced (terminated) to give the other vesicle and the mare the very best chance possible. A second ultrasound at 25 days will confirm a heartbeat on the new embryo, and is a very good sign that the pregnancy is progressing normally.

Ultrasounds on Miniature mares are not necessarily as readily available as they are for their larger cousins. Some veterinarians don't feel comfortable doing internal rectal ultrasounds on Miniatures, and this is the most definitive method for reproduction ultrasounds and pregnancy diagnosis, particularly at these early stages. Sometimes, veterinarians use a wand, an extension on the ultrasound probe, to be able to more comfortably ultrasound without rectal palpation. The size of your mare may also play a factor and you'll need to check your vet's comfort with the procedure.

A less scientific and conclusive option is to continue to tease your mare when you know she would be coming back into estrus, and when she doesn't come back in, there is a good possibility that she is pregnant. There is still the possibility that she just didn't like the stallion that cycle, or that she lost a pregnancy early on, which changed up her hormones and kept her from cycling for a time. But if you are okay with "most likely pregnant," this method is definitely the most affordable—and least invasive.

There are other options for pregnancy detection, which vary depending on how far along the mare is. Blood tests can check hormone levels, and are effective at certain points in the pregnancy, and urine tests are available to purchase online, again dependent on the point of gestation.

Preparing for Baby

For most of her pregnancy, your mare doesn't require any additional care or special management (fig. 13.8). She needs her usual maintenance diet to keep her healthy and happy, and she can continue doing whatever her usual job is, even if she is a hard-working, performance horse.

Vaccination and Deworming

For the most part, your mare can stay on her usual deworming and vaccination schedule. One vaccine that you may want to talk to your vet about (depending on your herd situation—that is, how many horses come and go) is the killed rhinopneumonitis vaccine, brand names Prodigy® or Pneumabort K®. Rhinopneumonitis, or "Rhino" for short, is a contagious respiratory disease in horses. However, some strains can cause neurological symptoms, and one strain can cause late-term abortions. Initially, your mare gets an upper respiratory infection—basically the common cold for horses—but then, at 9 to 11 months gestation, she loses her foal. This can be quite devastating in a herd of broodmares, potentially triggering what is known as "abortion storms" where each mare exposed to the virus may lose her foal. The vaccine for pregnant mares is the killed version, which is just a different way of preparing the virus than in the modified live vaccine. It should be administered at 5, 7, and 9 months gestation to provide the best protection. In some situations, veterinarians recommend vaccination at 3 months as well.

13.8 *Toybox Barbie Doll shows the big belly and rapidly shedding winter coat of late pregnancy.*

It is optimal for your mare to have her annual vaccinations two to four weeks prior to foaling so she has the best opportunity to build up these antibodies in the colostrum and can passes them on to her foal. She can be dewormed at this time too; any parasites in her system will be killed and shed before the foal comes into her environment.

Environmental Antibodies

It is a good idea to have your mare in the environment where she will foal, and where the foal will spend his first days, for at least a couple weeks prior to foaling. This allows her body to become accustomed to any little pathogens that might be in that environment (stall, barn, paddock) and develop antibodies that will then be in the colostrum to give the foal the best chance against any bugs in his new world (fig. 13.9).

Handling and Routine

Another reason to move your mare into her foaling environment early is to make her comfortable

13.9 *Mares due to foal are often stalled at night to keep them in a safe, easily monitored environment.*

with her new routine before the stress of parturition and new motherhood. If this means she is going to be stalled at night so she is easy to view on a camera, but she isn't usually stalled at all, this is going to be an adjustment, and the further away from foaling you start her new routine, the better she is going to feel about it by the time foal arrives.

During this time you can also get the mare used to some of the different handling you're going to require leading up to foaling. You will want to touch her udder, possibly attempt to milk a drop or two; and peek under her tail, and poke at the muscles around her tail head. You will need to feel her belly. Some mares are really not comfortable with all this, and you will all be happier if you can gradually help her become accustomed to it.

Feeding Requirements

It is during this last stage of pregnancy that you start increasing your mare's nutrition. A great way to do this is with a complete feed specifically designed for mares and foals. This way, not only will it give her all the extra nutrition she needs to start producing milk but will continue to be appropriate when the baby starts sharing her dam's dinner.

As it is likely that your mare is spending more time than usual in a stall, ensuring that she has a constant supply of roughage in the form of grass hay will help keep her stomach happy and healthy. As much turnout time as possible is also important. Even when my mares are very close to foaling, they are outdoors anytime I am home and it isn't nasty out. We've had mares that much prefer to foal outdoors and we are happy to accommodate them.

Chapter 14:
Foaling

When Will It Happen?

It is an old joke that the gestation of the mare is 11 months, 11 days, and 11 minutes after you check them, and it's definitely one of those "funny because it's true" situations.

So much of a horse's behavior is shaped by her evolution as a flight animal, and foaling is no exception. In the wild, the life of a mare and her foal depends on her not broadcasting to predators that she is about to foal. They come by their sneakiness honestly! Mares can even postpone foaling to some extent when they feel unsafe, so while you're watching her closely, do so from a quiet, unobtrusive distance so she feels comfortable and safe.

Chances are, everything will go well with your mare, but when things go wrong, they can go very wrong very quickly. That is why breeders spend spring time glued to a barn camera and are constantly sleep deprived!

When to Start "Mare Stare"

As we discussed in the previous chapter, the "official" gestation for a horse is 340 days, but more realistically, in many breeds a range of 320 to 360 would be considered within normal. And when we're talking Miniature Horses that span

gets even wider. We have had healthy, normal foals born all the way from 302 to 360 days, and I know of some that were over a year. That's a full two-month window, which means that even if you know your exact breeding date you still don't have a very good idea of when the foal will arrive. As I've said, we figure on an average of 320 days for a Miniature Horse. (Keep in mind, of course, that being average is not in a mare's vocabulary.)

Udder Development

We have a found a much more reliable predictor of foaling is udder development. We check every mare daily (or twice daily) once she is nearing 300 days so we are aware of every change in her udder. As soon as we find that she is "bagging up," that is when she goes into the barn at night and is carefully monitored. In most cases, mares don't foal until they have a large, hard udder—I always say if she's got a "corner" on her bag, then she's getting serious: when the udder gets very full there is an edge to it so it feels almost square. The position of the nipples can also be a guideline—usually if they're still pointing at each other, she's not quite ready, but as soon as they turn toward the ground it's almost show time.

Often, we've found that a maiden mare bags up a lot sooner than an experienced mare —with

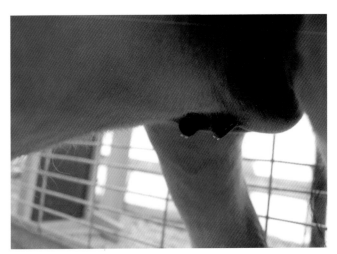

14.1 *In the hours prior to foaling, some mares will wax. Here is Dazzle with a large udder and wax about 12 hours before she foaled.*

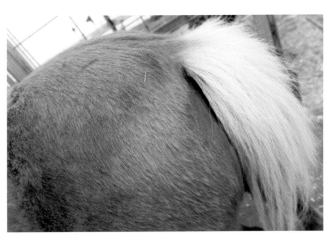

14.2 *As the muscles of the mare's hindquarters relax in preparation for foaling, her tail head will begin to look very "pointed" and prominent.*

an old experienced mare, as soon as she bags up, we watch her like a hawk because she sometimes doesn't bag up until the day of foaling.

That being said, there are always exceptions, and when you're talking about foaling mares, it can seem like exceptions outnumber the ones that follow the rules. To be safe, any mare over 300 days gestation needs to be monitored, regardless of udder development.

Waxing

In most breeds, the biggest and most reliable indicator of impending parturition is waxing. "Wax" is colostrum that leaks out and beads on the end of the nipple, and it looks very much like wax (fig. 14.1). Usually, once a mare starts waxing she will foal within 48 hours.

However, in over 30 years of foaling Miniature Horses, we have had very few that waxed before foaling, and even fewer who did so with every pregnancy, so if you wait for mare to wax before you start watching her closely, chances are very good that you will miss the big event.

Other Signs

There are other changes to the mare's body as she prepares to deliver, and how obvious these changes are will vary greatly depending on the mare. One of the first physical signs as your mare gets into late pregnancy is that she is often one of the first to start seriously shedding her winter coat.

The softening of the ligaments in her hindquarters is one of the more consistent signs, too, giving her tail head a more pointed look (fig. 14.2). If you gently poke the muscles around her tail, they will jiggle like Jell-O. The shape of her vulva will change as well, elongating as it relaxes.

"Has she dropped yet?" Someone might ask you this question when you're on foal watch. The idea is that as the mare gets close, her belly will "drop" getting lower as the foal starts to get into position. What we have found to be a more likely sign is when you turn her out one morning and she hardly looks pregnant anymore, as if the belly is gone. These are the days we don't leave her alone.

Mares are very sneaky and can foal very quickly. Remember, the best way to find a foal is when he is up and dry and nursing, so don't feel bad for missing the action when this is the result. We've had mares demanding their breakfast one minute and, by the time the rest of the horses had been fed, produced a foal. We've had mares refusing to foal in the barn and waiting until they are turned out. And we've often had mares foal that we thought still had some time to go and weren't even under the camera yet.

Helpful Tools

Barn Cameras

Having a camera in your barn can be an actual lifesaver (fig. 14.3). When I was in college, we slept in the barn with the foaling mares, which was lots of fun, but we had our friends, cots, and a loft that looked down into the stalls. A camera lets you keep that same close eye on your mare from the comfort of your own bed. My current camera setup is a simple D-Link® camera (or two) that I can access using an app on my smartphone. This means that on a day I have to be away from the farm I can still monitor the mares from wherever I am, and I can share the link with family and friends. More eyes mean more chances that someone will be looking at the right time and can call the person who is closest to get there and help.

Along those lines, there are online services with large communities of people who will help you monitor your mare around the clock. They'll see the live video from your barn with your phone number underneath so when anything happens, they can let you know. Not everyone is comfortable with that level of public access to their private barn, but many people have great success and credit the online community with saving the life of their foal. This also might be an excellent option when you are new to foaling, because it

14.3 These readily available cameras make it easy for me to monitor my mares from my smart phone.

gives you access to more experienced advice, or at least, lots of advice and constant monitoring.

Alarm Systems

There are systems you can purchase to alert you when the mare lies down flat out (as she does when foaling). One goes on her halter and sends a signal to a beeper or your phone as soon as she lies down. Another goes around her torso like a surcingle and performs similarly. The downfall of systems like these is that mares often lie down in lateral recumbency when they are not foaling, so it works best as a tool used in conjunction with a camera. This way, when the beeper goes off, you check the camera and see if there really is something goes on, or if she's just having a nice snooze or rubbing her chin on the fence.

There is another form of alarm that is a magnetic device that is sutured into the vulva of the mare by a veterinarian. When the membranes or feet of the foal emerge, the magnet is pulled apart and sets off the alarm. This is less likely to have false alarms, but it is possible for the mare to rub the magnet out, and it isn't unheard of for

Miniature Tales
Barbie

I am able to access my barn cameras from my phone, so I can watch the mares from my warm bed, or wherever I happen to be, a feature that came in handy when I had a doctor's appointment in the city on a day when I was already wondering what Barbie was waiting for.

I checked her before I left, and she had a big, hard, easily milked bag, but was eating and seemed very relaxed, so I was optimistic she might wait until I got home.

I called and warned Grandma that I was leaving; we are only about 10 minutes from her house, so she and Grandad were on alert in case I needed them to race over.

As soon as I got to my appointment, I checked

14.4 Newborn baby "Up" figured out nursing shortly after I got home. Healthy and happy: Good job, Barbie!

my phone and watched Barbie eating while I waited my turn to see the doctor. Driving home, I realized that I had forgotten my house key and had to make a detour to my mom's work to get her key. She asked how Barbie was and I said, "Oh, she seems okay, has been eating mostly," as I got my phone out to look again, only to see her stand up, turn around and immediately go down again. Red alert!

I ran across the parking lot to my car, called Grandma, and raced for home, my phone with the live feed on the steering wheel. Traffic in our town is notoriously bad, and if you happened to be in Cochrane on that May afternoon I was the crazy lady at the red light waving her phone around and shouting, "Yay, it's alive!" as soon as I saw the baby move on his own.

I parked haphazardly outside the barn gate, and ran in to discover the new colt, sitting up on his chest, Barbie still down and nickering at her new baby. Dazzle, the maiden mare in the next stall, was standing with splayed legs as she tried to figure out how that thing got into Barbie's stall. My grandparents arrived right behind me and we watched as the foal took his first steps and learned to nurse (fig. 14 4).

While in this case, Barbie had everything well in hand and didn't need me at all, the fact that I was able to watch on the camera and know it was time to get home gave me a great peace of mind. When mares need help, they need it fast, and if things hadn't appeared to be going well I could have had the vet on the way before I even got home. I highly recommend a camera for anyone who is foaling out a mare.

the mare to foal without triggering the alarm.

All these tools are just that, tools that may help you be there when your mare needs you, but there are no guarantees. One of my mares once waited until the day I was at work, the internet was down, and my brother ran a quick errand to town, to deliver a healthy colt all by herself.

Milk Test Strips

Many people have good luck using milk test strips, or standard pH test strips, to help predict foaling. Again, it's not going to be 100 percent accurate, and some mares aren't able to be milked prior to foaling, but it is another tool. You just need a few drops of milk and the strips test the calcium and pH and give you a range of time until foaling based on the color the strip changes to. It's a simple test to do, with the added bonus that it gets your mare more accustomed to having her udder handled before the foal arrives.

Other Preparation

Turnout and Exercise

There has been some speculation that the increased incidence we see in dystocia (difficult birth) in all horses, but Miniature Horses, in particular, can be in part due to our management of them. Horses are designed to move, and even though it makes it much easier for us to monitor them when they are in a stall, it's often not the best situation for the mare. This is why it's my preference to allow the mare as much turnout as possible, with space to move around and stretch her muscles. It isn't uncommon for mares that are heavy in foal and confined to a stall to develop ventral edema, which is swelling on her belly, or to stock up, which is swelling of the limbs. When you are stalling your mare 24/7, she needs to be

"Breeding stock must have sweet, quiet personalities. They must have correct conformation, be refined, and look like full-sized horse. There shouldn't be evidence of known dwarfism in their background. No health issues. If a mare or stallion does not meet these standards then don't breed them!"

Joyce Ebert R.V.T,. WalkingBear Farm Miniature Performance Horses and Training Center

hand-walked several times a day. Giving birth is a very physical activity, and a mare that has spent the previous month in a stall has lost a lot of muscle tone, making her job much harder.

Grooming

First, since Miniature Horses grow an unbelievable amount of winter hair, and, second, foaling season generally coincides with shedding season, many people routinely do a "broodmare clip" prior to foaling to made the udder more accessible to the newborn foal, and minimize the risk of the foal sucking on and ingesting hair. All the area around the udder, under her belly, and over the mare's flanks is clipped, still leaving her with most of her coat so she will be warm and comfortable. However, if your mare has never been clipped, the stress of the process may outweigh the benefits. In this case, just be sure your mare stays well groomed (no matting as she sheds and frequent brushing out of loose hair) and that you are there to monitor the foal as he learns to suck, and clear any hair from his eyes and mouth.

14.5 *Having a blanket on hand for your foal is a good idea regardless of the time of year or your local climate.*

Miniature Tales
Bunny

Martin's Bunny was one of our first three Miniature Horses, and she went on to become the foundation broodmare of our herd. She was a great mom, very protective of her baby. And as part of that protectiveness, she felt that it was her solemn duty to ensure that no one got to see her foal. Bunny was very sneaky, and her best work was the time my grandad turned her out of the barn in the morning, fed her breakfast, which she was noisily demanding and dug right into, and then carried on with feeding the rest of the herd. A few short minutes later the hired man came out of the barn looking for Grandad, caught up with him and asked, "Is Bunny's foal a filly or a colt?" She had to have barely waited for Grandad to turn his back before she lay down and foaled.

Baby Blankets

In the first few days of life a foal isn't able to consistently regulate his own body temperature and you may need to help him stay warm—or cool—depending on your climate. Here, we always have warm winter foal blankets available; even summer foals can be shivery and need a little extra layer at night (fig. 14.5). Use caution when introducing the blanket as some mares won't recognize their foal with a blanket on. It can help to show her the blanket first then see you putting it on the foal; rubbing the outside of the blanket on the foal to pick up his smell can make a difference, as well.

It's Time!

First Stage Labor

When you've been watching your mare for days and nights on end, you'll get used to her normal routine. Classic signs of early labor include pacing, pawing, biting at sides, shifting weight, rubbing hind legs together, yawning, lip curling, not eating, loose manure, frequent urination, any sign of discomfort. The trouble is that these things can also be signs of boredom, or itchiness from a shedding coat, for example. The biggest sign to watch for is anything out of the ordinary—a change in behavior. I watched an Arabian mare that had been picking at her feed for two weeks, and the night that she cleaned up every speck of her hay and kept eating when we gave her more was the night that she foaled.

First stage labor can go on for hours or be just a flip of her tail before her water breaks. This labor amounts to early contractions as the mare's body gets ready for delivery, and it will vary greatly with every mare. Often mares do follow a similar pattern with subsequent foals though, so it's worth

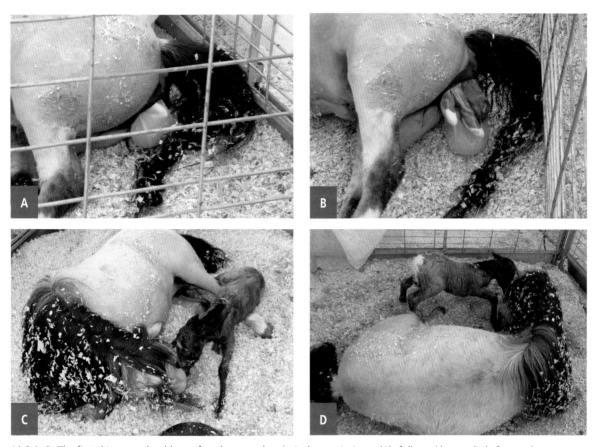

14.6 A–D The first thing you should see after the water breaks is the amniotic sac (A), followed by two little feet and a little nose (B). Dazzle meets her new baby girl (C)! Little Downy tries out her legs for the very first time (D).

making some notes if you are planning to rebreed her in the future.

Water Breaking

The end of first stage labor is marked by the water breaking. After that, things should happen fast, and when they don't, you need to either be prepared to step in and help, or get a veterinarian on the way. While it might cost you, it's far better to have the vet arrive just in time to do a checkup on a healthy foal that the mare ended up delivering on her own, than it is to have waited too long and be unable to save one or the other. When she isn't making progress after 20 minutes, it's time to act.

The foal should be out within 30 minutes, and if it's not, it is an emergency.

Mares will often get up and down—sometimes quite dramatically—during the delivery of the foal, but most foals are delivered with the mare lying flat on her side. Occasionally, a mare will stand while she delivers—try to catch the foal and cushion the fall when this is the case.

The first thing you should see after the water breaks is the amniotic sac—it's a whitish bubble with some fluid in it (figs. 14.6 A). Next, you'll be able to see the feet and they should come out one slightly ahead of the other, followed by the nose (fig. 14.6 B). The head isn't usually a trouble spot in a big horse, but sometimes it's a tight squeeze for a Miniature and your mare might appreciate a little assistance. The shoulders can also be a tight fit. If you decide to help pull the foal, pull only when the mare is pushing, and pull down toward her hind feet. As soon as baby's head is clear, you can remove the sac from the head and run your hand down his face to help clear his nostrils. Most foals will start shaking their head, trying to sit up on their chest and even nickering even before they're completely out in the world (figs. 14.6 C & D).

A "Red Bag" Emergency

If the first thing you see is a dark red bubble, you have a "red bag" delivery and you need to act now. A red bag means that the placenta has already detached and your foal isn't getting any oxygen. You can still save your baby: cut through the rubbery red placenta, find the foal's feet and deliver the foal as quickly as you can.

There are all sorts of presentation issues that can hinder delivery, and unless you have experience, it's probably best to have a good equine veterinarian on call. As I've mentioned already, whenever foaling isn't progressing quickly—remember foaling should happen *fast*—and if anything seems out of the ordinary, err on the side of caution and

get your vet on the phone. Trust me, the vet would rather have to talk you through something that is completely normal than have you not call soon enough to be able to save the life of your mare and foal. When in doubt, call your vet.

Bonding Time

Once the foal is delivered, if all seems well and you have an active, breathing foal, I like to pull the foal forward, across the mare's hind legs. This not only brings him close enough that momma can reach to visit and encourage her to stay down long enough to allow all the valuable placental blood to reach the foal, but when she does get up, the foal will slide safely off her back legs rather than ending up under her feet.

This is the time to get out of the stall—maybe after a very quick peek to determine if you have a filly or a colt. This is an important bonding time for mom and baby. Let them get to know each other and let the mare feel safe to stay down while she rests and before the cord breaks. Now is when you get to catch your breath and lean on the stall wall and admire what is no doubt the cutest, prettiest, most perfect baby you ever saw in your life. I know mine always are!

Umbilical Cord

When the mare gets to her feet, the umbilical cord generally breaks. There is a spot on the cord near the foal's belly that constricts. When the cord doesn't break—we've found newborn foals walking around dragging the whole placenta with them—the first thing to try is to lay the foal down, support his belly wall with your hand, and apply some pressure on the cord. Don't jerk on it or pull too hard, but sometimes a little tension is all it needs to let go. If not, you can tie it off and cut it.

"Have a plan for what will happen when it is time to foal out your mare. If you're not prepared for either the time investment to watch the mare yourself or the financial investment to have the mare at a facility or vet clinic to foal out, it doesn't make sense to breed in the first place."

Dr. Crystal Lee, Burwash Equine Services

The umbilical stump is a very likely avenue of infection. For years it was common practice to treat the navel with iodine after birth, but more recent studies have found that the caustic effects of iodine can do more harm than good. In addition to keeping the foal in a clean environment, it is advised to treat the navel with dilute chlorhexidine (4:1 dilution with water) three times daily for three days following birth.

Standing, Nursing, and Pooping

When Not to Help

One of the best parts of foaling season is standing outside the stall watching a newborn foal learn to stand and walk. Resist the urge to help him. Instead, remove any pails or other obstacles from the stall; it is normal for him to crash around a bit and fall. Bed him deep and don't worry about him; as long as he is trying, he will figure it out. You won't actually do him any favors by getting in there and putting him on his feet. His struggles to stand are part of what gets his new systems functioning.

Colostrum Matters

He needs to have a good suck, ideally within an hour. If he isn't nursing by two or three hours after he's born, it is time for veterinary involvement. By the time he is 12 hours old, he has lost most of the ability to absorb the valuable antibodies in the colostrum, and he needs as much of these as possible if he's going to thrive (fig. 14.7).

Teaching foals to nurse is the single most frustrating thing on the planet. They naturally push against pressure and refuse to be guided. Resisting the urge to get in there for the first little while is probably the best thing you can do for him. Get out of his way. The exception might be when the foal is too weak to search for the teat on his own

14.7 All dried off and fluffed up at 12 hours old.

14.8 As a maiden mare, Dazzle was a bit worried about both letting her new baby out of her sight and allowing her to nurse. It took some time and patience until they both figured it out.

or doesn't have a good suckle reflex (in which case you need a vet), or when the mare—particularly a maiden—is too worried about where he is to stand still enough to allow him to find the milk bar. In this case, holding the mare's halter might help him out (fig. 14.8).

Meconium

After he has a good meal—or sometimes, even before—the foal will pass the meconium, which is the first manure. It's a tarry sticky poop that can sometimes cause some issues for them. Colts, especially, can have difficulty passing it and need an enema to help things move along. You can use a Fleet® enema from your drug store. If you notice he is straining a lot, or if he starts displaying colic symptoms, you need to consult your vet.

Placenta

The placenta and the membranes of the amniotic sac won't usually pass at the same time as the foal is delivered and your mare will walk around

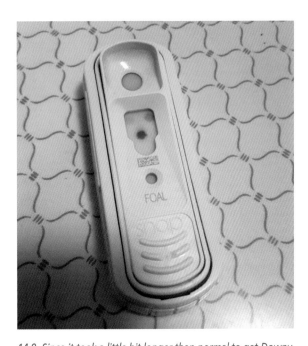

14.9 Since it took a little bit longer than normal to get Downy to nurse, 12 hours later we drew blood for a SNAP test to check her IgG levels. Luckily, it showed that she got all the antibodies she needed and all was well. Your vet will perform this test using your foal's blood—when the blue dot at the bottom is brighter than the one on the upper left, it indicates your foal has adequate passive transfer of antibodies.

dragging them while she looks after her new foal. You can tie the membranes in knots to keep her from stepping on them, and to help gravity do its part to remove the placenta. Never pull on the placenta as that can tear it and leave a chunk in the uterus. Usually the placenta passes within the first hour, often once the foal sucks and causes her uterus to start to contract.

If it doesn't pass within a couple hours, three at the most, you need to be in contact with your veterinarian. A retained placenta can be a life-threatening situation for a mare; when the tissue starts to rot inside her uterus it can cause an infection that can quickly go systemic. Mares with retained placentas are also at high risk of developing laminitis. Your vet will have drugs and procedures to help things along.

If you are planning a routine vet call for a checkup, save the placenta for the vet to check. If not, lay it out and take a look at it: there should be only one hole in it, where the foal came out, and you should be able to find the tips of both the pregnant and non-pregnant horn. Any changes in the texture or color should be noted and discussed with your vet, and when there is more than one hole your mare needs to be examined.

IgG and Vet Check

It's a good idea in general, but especially if you have any concerns about how much colostrum your foal got, to have the vet out to do a checkup at 24 hours old. The vet will check for issues like congenital eye problems (cataracts), limb deformities, cleft palate, and look at the umbilicus. The vet will also draw blood to test the antibody levels in the foal's blood. It's a simple quick test performed at stall side, but when the foal fails to receive immunity (not receive enough antibodies from the colostrum), he is very likely to contract a life-threatening infection so it's a good idea to give him an infusion of plasma. When the blood test is normal, you know you have the best chance for a healthy baby (fig. 14.9).

First Days

What to Watch For: The Mare

Your mare should be bright and alert, interested in her foal, and eating and drinking normally almost as soon as she catches her breath. She might not pass manure for a bit, as she probably cleared out before and during foaling, but within 12 hours she should be back to normal. If she has anything but a bit of watery bloody discharge, such as thick, purulent, or smelly drainage from her vulva, she needs to be seen by a vet. Watch her for signs of colic; many mares are quite "crampy" post foaling and may need a little pain killer from your vet to help them feel better.

What to Watch For: The Foal

Your foal should eat, sleep, and play in almost equal amounts. If you notice he is always sucking, maybe he isn't getting as much milk as he needs. He should also sleep in a "shrimp" position, on his side with his forelimbs curled up. A foal that sleeps like this is a content foal. Monitor your baby closely his first days for any signs of lethargy, diarrhea, or lameness. In a newborn, all three of these are dangerous and generally require hospitalization. A foal that is rolling up on his back is showing symptoms of colic and needs the vet.

At around 10 days old, many foals will have "foal-heat diarrhea," softer feces as the diet changes with the mare's hormones as she goes through her first estrus cycle following pregnancy. This is to be expected, but it is essential that the foal remains otherwise bright and healthy, and if you have any concerns you should definitely consult the vet.

Turnout

Once the new mom and foal are well bonded and the foal has all the basics figured out, it's time to

Dystocia and Abortion

It is a common perception that Miniature Horses have more difficulty delivering than full-sized horses. I'm not sure it is entirely true, but it is absolutely true that when things do go wrong, it is a lot harder to fix because there is so little room to work. A dystocia (difficult birth) can lose you not only your foal, but your mare as well.

I do think that, anecdotally anyway, Miniature Horses have a much higher incidence of abortion. I suspect this is in some part due to the prevalence of dwarfism, but there may be other factors as well, as I know of many mares that have difficulty carrying to term. While there are options you can try that may help (hormones, for example), with the mare in my herd that never carried a foal to term, I chose to stop breeding her. I don't want to risk something happening to her just for the sake of a foal.

Did I scare you yet? While it's important to know the risks so you can deal with them properly if they arise, you will probably have a normal delivery and a healthy foal. But if you don't feel you are equipped to give your mare the care and attention she needs, most equine veterinary clinics are willing to foal out client mares, and what better place for your foal to be born than with the people who know just how to keep him healthy and happy?

start getting them out of the stall. Foals need to get out and stretch their legs to continue to gain strength, and fresh air is much better for little lungs than even the cleanest stall. Begin with a short, well supervised outing—a great chance to get your first outdoor photos—and gradually work up to them spending the whole day outside. By the time your foal is a week old, provided they have access to shelter from the elements, they can be outside most or all of the time (fig. 14.10).

14.10 Little Up enjoying his first turnout time, and running his worried mom, Barbie, quite ragged.

14.11 Up and Downy playing together in the big pasture. Room to play and stretch their legs is important for building healthy, strong bones and joints.

It is best, especially for the first week of life, for the mare and foal to be in a private pen. Until they are very well bonded, the foal is following the mare well, and she is showing a good protective instinct, you don't want to introduce other horses to the mix. When you do, make sure that they are introduced carefully, with lots of space for everyone to get away and ample shelter space so baby isn't kept out in the rain by a more dominant adult. Supervise any introductions very carefully so that aggressive horses can be removed from the space (fig. 14.11).

Foal-Safe Fences

While Miniature Horses require more secure fencing than a regular-sized horse does, foals need even more of a careful approach. Miniature foals are, well, very miniature. I have seen a foal trot right through a standard stock panel without even breaking stride. Check your gates, as distance between bars and the hinge gap between gate and post can potentially be enough space for a foal to slip through—or worse, get caught. This fence check is best done prior to foaling, and it is a good idea to keep any mares that are close to foaling in extra secure fencing. It is not uncommon to hear stories of mares who foaled "under the fence" so the newborn foal got up on the wrong side of the barrier and wasn't able to get to his dam for the critical first milk and protection.

As an added benefit of this careful fence check, any fence secure enough to contain a tiny, newborn Miniature Horse is likely also secure enough to keep your newborn Miniature Horse safe from predators. While his dam will do her best to protect her foal, her small size can make them vulnerable. Depending on your location, the biggest danger may be neighborhood dogs or coyotes that can be kept out by secure fencing. If larger predators, such as cougars or bears, are common in your area, keeping your foal inside at night for a more prolonged time would be appropriate.

Bringing Up Baby

Foals need lots of socialization, both from their dam and other herd members, and from humans. What they don't need, at least in the early stages, is lots of training. Studies have shown that the best way to acclimatize foals to becoming calm with general handling is to give them lots of chances to see their dam being handled, showing them that it is a calm, relaxed, and normal way for horses to behave during haltering, leading, and grooming.

Socialize your foal gradually. Spend time grooming his dam, or sitting in their stall or pasture. Foals are very curious and they will come up to see what you are up to if you display just a bit of patience (fig. 14.12). Foals are also itchy creatures, so the way to their heart is always through a good scratch. As part of your scratching, cuddling, and playtime, start very gently and slowly handling their legs, teaching them to pick up their feet and allow them to get used to wearing a halter.

Remember, just because you can outmuscle a foal and drag him on a halter to where you need him, doesn't mean that is the right way to teach him to lead, and it definitely isn't the right way to gain his trust and make him excited to come and play with you again the next day. Halter training is best undertaken once the foal is at least a month old but before they are weaned. Beginning by allowing the foal to follow his dam to get the idea of leading will make everything much less traumatic for him (fig. 14.13).

Be warned that some foals react very dramatically to their first haltering sessions, and you need

14.12 Early socialization of foals should be lots of calm visiting and scratching. Little Downy loved it when new people came to visit her.

to be careful to keep them safe. As they are so small, it is easy for them to throw themselves over backward, with some serious danger of head trauma should they land poorly. Taking your time, getting them used to small steps, keeping their mother close at hand, and working in a stall or small space at first, will make it much less traumatic.

While keeping training sessions short is always a horse-training rule to live by, when you are talking about foals they really need to be quick. Foals don't have the mental energy to work on a lesson for more than a few minutes at a time. Start and finish a few moments of leading practice with lots of scratching and hanging out so that it's always a positive experience.

Foal Hoof and Health Care

Foals will need to have their feet trimmed much more often than adult horses. Frequent trimming—every four weeks or so, but this can vary depending on your foal—will prevent overgrown hooves from twisting still developing legs, and if your foal has

14.13 *With just a few gentle halter lessons under his belt, at six months of age, Up leads with confidence.*

any minor limb issues, proper trims by an experienced farrier can help to correct them and encourage his legs to grow straight and strong.

Deworming is an important part of foal husbandry. Foals should be dewormed beginning at two months of age, and then every two months until they are a year old, usually alternating with fendbendazole and pyrantel, but make a plan with your veterinarian to determine what the best choices are for your area and situation. Waiting too long to begin a proper deworming protocol can have serious consequences for your baby foal.

If your mare was vaccinated prior to foaling, your foal will have a good immunity from antibodies he received through the colostrum. His first vaccines should be given at six months of age, and he will need a booster in two to four weeks. Once the initial series has been completed, an annual booster will ensure protection through his lifetime. Which vaccines your foal needs will depend on your situation and location. Once again, confer with your veterinarian to make a plan that is right for your foal.

Shedding vs. Clipping

Foals are often born with a thick fuzzy coat, especially if they are born early or late in the year. It is a commonly held belief that foals won't shed on their own and will need to be body clipped, but foals will shed their foal coat in the summer time, perhaps not as slick as an adult horse, but they will shed. In hot climates, you may want to clip your foal to help him stay cool, but in most cases, you won't need to. The foal coat will not only protect them from weather, but also from bugs, sun, and other irritants. Most often the reason people clip their foals is to see them all shined up, or to promote them for sales. Keep in mind that when you take away the foal's natural protection through body clipping, it becomes your responsibility to take care of all the things that their coat is meant to do.

Supplemental Feed

Your mare's nutritional requirements increase dramatically as she is nursing a foal, and continue to increase as the foal grows. Soon the baby will be able to eat some solid food as well, and feeding them both a good quality mare-and-foal extruded feed ensures they have all the nutrition they need. It's also good for baby to be accustomed to eating his grain ration prior to weaning to reduce the stress for him.

I like to allow the foals to learn to be horses before they have to learn to do what I want them to do. Of course, I spend time with them, scratching, playing, and just generally hanging out, but I would rather they got to be babies and watch mom be handled and play with their buddies and run and grow strong before I ask them to wear a halter or lead.

Chapter 15:
Weaning, Castration, and Marketing

Time for Weaning

The quality of the mare's milk decreases quite a bit around the third month of lactation, so in the past, breeders took that as a cue that three months was an appropriate time for weaning. Further research on equine ethology has shown that while the foal gets less nutrition from their dam's milk after three months, they still benefit both from the feeding and, even more greatly, from the relationship.

More current studies suggest it is best to wean your foals at not less than six months of age.

"I adore large horses, but I connect more with the little ones in a very deep way. I feel less stressed and am more relaxed when I spend time with them. I am less worried about getting hurt and even my non-horsey friends and family feel more comfortable being around them. They are so much more accessible to children, fearful adults and even people with special needs. Time with my Miniature Horses is better than therapy!"

Tina Silva, Crickhollow Farm

Depending on the foal, he may benefit from further time with his dam, but six to nine months is a good window. Watch for signs of independence, spending more time with other members of the herd, and eating well.

Some people choose to wean the foal when he starts "pulling down" the mare and she begins to lose body condition. It makes sense that feeding a big, growing, active foal will be hard work for her. For this job, you need to make sure she has the proper nutrition to feed both. As the foal gets bigger, monitor the mare's condition carefully and increase her ration as needed to help her out, and allow the foal to get the full benefit of his dam's feeding and care as long as he needs it.

Minimizing Stress

Even when you have a big, healthy, independent foal over the age of six months, it is still going to be traumatic to remove him from the biggest relationship of his life. There are several different schools of thought regarding weaning. Studies have found that foals show the least elevation in their stress hormone when they are separated from nursing, but are still able to see, smell, hear, and even touch their mother through a safe and secure fence. By

15.1 *Weaning day is much less stressful for moms, babies, and caretakers when the foals are at least six months of age, eating well, and are able to see, hear and even touch their dams through a safe, secure fence. Barbie and her eight-month-old colt, Up, visit through the fence shortly after weaning.*

this age, much of the comfort they derive from their dam is simply in her presence, and being able to know she is close by will make everything less stressful for both of them (fig. 15.1).

Some people like to do a "gradual" weaning, where the foal is separated overnight and back with the dam through the day, or vice versa. This is actually going to make it much more difficult on both mare and foal, as they just worry over and over again, but especially the mare. It is very uncomfortable for the mare when her udder fills up as the foal no longer drinks. By repeatedly allowing the foal back in to nurse, she continues to make more milk and she doesn't begin the process of drying up. To help the process along, don't allow the foal to drink, and don't milk her out, even if it feels like it will make her more comfortable. Instead, stop feeding her any grain until she

is dried up, put her where she can see her foal so she doesn't stress, and encourage her to move around; putting her in with new friends to help distract her and convince her to get some exercise is a good idea as well.

Foals also do better with a friend. Sometimes when small breeders have only one foal to wean, they arrange to work with another small breeder so the babies can be weaning buddies. If they don't have another foal for them to live with, then an older horse often makes a good babysitter, keeping the youngster company and continuing the work the dam did to teach him to be a good equine citizen.

It is important to do what you can to minimize the stress of weaning. Foals are at the highest risk of getting sick immediately post weaning, and a stress-filled weaning can also impact their growth.

Feeding for Growth

Once the foal is weaned, you become 100 percent responsible for his health. Remember that growing babies need a lot of nutrition. Sometimes people get worried about their future show horse getting too fat his first year, and try to restrict his feed, or simply are fooled by his impressively woolly first winter coat and don't realize he is too thin.

Weanlings should be fed a diet of free-choice roughage, as well as a commercial complete feed specifically formulated for young growing horses. Don't worry about your foal being too fat—the best way to begin to condition a future show yearling is to feed him lots of good quality feed as a weanling. Put your hands on him frequently and check for condition.

If you notice your foal has a big belly, this can be a warning sign he isn't getting enough. Make sure you can't easily feel his ribs, hips, and backbone. A distended belly can be a sign of a lack of protein in the diet of a growing horse or general malnutrition. Think of pictures you may have seen of starving children—they often have a distended belly. Also double-check that your deworming protocol is effective.

Horses do 75 percent of their growing in their first year. Just like a teenage boy in a growth spurt

"Miniature Horses are much tougher than my big horses when it comes to weather and horsing around, but they are more sensitive when it comes to my emotions."

Jessica Willis, JLR Farm

who is always hungry, weanling and yearling Miniature Horses need a lot of nutrition to grow to their best potential.

Castration

Unless you have a colt or stallion of exceptional quality, with traits you wish to use to produce exceptional foals for a carefully planned purpose, and you have the skill and knowledge to properly handle, train, promote, and care for a stallion, you need to geld him. Geldings are not only easier to deal with from a training and management standpoint, but they also live a more social and less stressful life than a stallion. Choosing to geld is a good choice for your horse as well.

Young Colts

The minor surgery involved in castration is much easier on young horses. They tend to recover very quickly with a minimum of swelling, and they have less carryover stallion behavior than a mature horse. Some Miniature Horses can be slow to have both testicles descend, but as soon as they have, the colt can be gelded, though it is best to wait until they are six months old and up-to-date with their tetanus vaccination. Speak to your vet about preferred timing. It's best not to do the surgery during peak fly season, and your colt will require some follow-up care, primarily regular exercise, so you need to be available in the week or two following the procedure.

Cryptorchidism (retained testicles) are not uncommon in Miniature Horses. When you have a colt with an undescended testicle, a little more time and age might resolve the issue so he can be gelded normally, or he might require a much more invasive surgery to remove the testicle from

"The Miniature Horse's temperament and level-headed approach to life is phenomenal."

Sherry Wilson McEwen, Carousel Miniatures

higher up in his abdomen. A horse with only one descended testicle should never be used for breeding because it can be a congenital condition, passed on to offspring. Retained testicles can also become cancerous or cause other issues for the horse, so they do need to be removed.

The descended testicle should never be removed without removing the undescended testicle as well. Retained testicles, although they cannot produce sperm due to the higher intra-abdominal temperature, still produce testosterone, so the horse will still behave like a stallion in every situation.

Older Stallions

Mature stallions can also be gelded at nearly any time, though there are more concerns for adult stallions as they have more blood flow to the area. Adult stallions often have more swelling and discomfort post-surgery than a youngster. Under your veterinarian's direction, you need to be extra vigilant in their exercise, and they may require a few days of anti-inflammatory treatment to help them feel a bit better as they heal. With a horse of any age, the peak of swelling and stiffness is usually around three to seven days post-surgery.

Stallions can have viable sperm for four to six weeks following the castration surgery, so any recently gelded stallions and colts still need to be kept separate from mares until after that time to ensure no accidental breeding occurs.

Benefits for You

Geldings are usually much easier to manage, both in housing situations, as they can live in a herd, unlike stallions, and in training. Stallions have the biological imperative of reproduction in the forefront of their mind at all times, making it very difficult for them to focus on what you are asking of them. Their traditional role in the herd as protector can also give them a constant split attention as they scan for danger and challenge any horse that may be a risk to their "herd."

You will quickly find it is much more peaceful, not to mention quieter, when you have one less stallion on the property.

It isn't unusual to see a colt offered for sale as a stallion, because his breeders find it "too expensive" to geld their colt prior to sale. There is always a 50/50 chance that the foal you produce will be a colt, and a 99 percent chance that the resulting colt will make a much better gelding than a stallion. If you feel the costs of castration are prohibitive, then seriously reconsider producing that foal in the first place.

Benefits for Your Horse

Stallions often lead quite a lonely existence. With their aggressiveness to other male horses, and the risk of pregnancy with female horses, they are often kept in isolation for their own well-being. Once he has been gelded and enough time has passed for him to adjust to the new lower levels of hormones, most stallions integrate well in a herd and very much enjoy the interaction with other horses (fig. 15.2).

It can be pretty common for owners to resist gelding their horse out of empathy for him, but this is misguided. Modern castration surgery is done with a minimum of stress for the horse, and

15.2 Geldings are able to live in a social herd of horses, a much more beneficial environment than that of a stallion that most often must be segregated. Hawk and Ruble enjoy some mutual grooming, one of many benefits of a herd-based environment.

he recovers very quickly. Your stallion will thank you when he is a happy, relaxed, well-adjusted gelding.

Marketing Your Horses

While, ideally, you are raising foals for yourself first, the reality is that if you are raising foals, then you'll ultimately be offering at least a portion of them for sale. Even if you don't raise foals of your own, there is a good chance that a horse will come into your life that isn't perfect for you, and a sale to the right home would be a much better option.

How to effectively sell those horses, getting back at least a portion of what you have invested in them, and do everything you can to ensure they have a home with an acceptable standard of care for the remainder of their days—well, that is the tricky part. There is no way to guarantee the well-being of the horse once he leaves your possession, but there are a number of things you can do to improve his chances.

Plan Before You Breed

As I touched on earlier, looking toward the future of your foal starts before he is even conceived. Is this cross going to be likely to produce a foal with the qualities you are looking for? Correct conformation, athletic ability, temperament? Is he going to be marketable? While registration papers certainly don't guarantee the quality of the horse, they do offer more options for future homes, and

15.3 *Horses with good ground manners that are easy to catch and handle for general management, are more likely to be properly cared for. Here Valdez stands quietly for the farrier, making it easy to ensure he has appropriate hoof care.*

more traceability, so you will have a better chance of following the horse throughout his lifetime.

Give Your Horse Skills

Auctions are full of unhandled young (and not so young) Miniature Horses. Giving your horse the basic handling skills to make him a good citizen is the least you can to give him an edge. Someone who is shopping for a horse is much more likely to choose the one that is easy to catch, groom,

"Miniature Horse? Strong personality in a little package."

Marsha Cloutier

and pick up his feet than one that is going to require a pile of time and effort to get to that point (fig. 15.3).

Beyond basic handling and life skills, the more training you can put into your horse, the more marketable he will be. Even if the potential buyer doesn't intend to do Obstacle or Agility with him, showing that he has the needed temperament and trainability will make him more appealing. Spending a little time to teach him something new, cleaning him up, and getting a good video of him showing his skills, and sharing that with your online advertising could be the way you find his new person.

One of the skills you can teach your horse is to drive. There are always more people looking for well-trained driving horses than there are well-trained driving horses available. If you have the time and money to invest in his training, it will pay off when finding him a home. But it does have to be done properly; too many Miniature Horses are started in harness simply by hooking them to a cart and hoping for the best. This approach is not fair to the horse and will almost never result in the happy and safe driving horse that buyers are looking for.

If you don't have the knowledge or time to do a proper job of driving training, sending him out to a qualified trainer might be a good option. Remember though, that all trainers are not created equal, and just because they offer Miniature Horse driving training does not mean that they are qualified to do so. Do some research, ask for references, speak to former clients—anything you can do to ensure you get the right person to care for and train your horse.

Advertising

You might have the most marketable horse in the area, but if you don't advertise, no one will know what you have. Luckily in this internet age, it is easy and often free to promote your sale horses. Facebook is a great venue, particularly to reach other Miniature Horse enthusiasts, as there are many large communities on Facebook dedicated to Miniatures. You can find a group specifically for promoting Miniature Horses for sale in your area, and you can cultivate your own network as well.

When promoting your horse on any social media, it's important to make your followers feel like a part of the horse's life. If they have had the opportunity to follow that horse through your posts from the day he was born, or the day he came onto your farm, see him grow, learn, and develop, see his ups and downs, then they are already invested in him. When you list him for sale, those people who have enjoyed the journey with you are going to be more likely to feel like the horse is already a member of their family.

To reach those who aren't on Facebook, a website for your horse makes it easier to find when people are searching for Miniature Horses in your area. You can advertise on your local Craigslist or Kijiji, as well as websites such as EquineNow or DreamHorse, all for free.

Join your local Miniature Horse club; most often they have a regular publication, whether print or online, where you can advertise horses for sale directly to other Miniature Horse people (fig. 15.4).

One of the very best ways to promote your

"Miniature Horses seem to have a ton of that mysterious thing called 'heart' and are (in general) so willing to do anything!"

Brenda Glowinski, Glowinski Miniature Horse Supplies

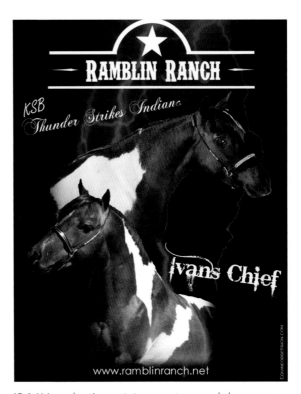

15.4 *Using advertisements to promote your sale horses or breeding program can make you more visible and accessible to potential buyers.*

horse for sale is to attend shows and events with him. Again, it is more of an investment of time and money, but it is the best marketing there is. In addition to getting your horse more experience and adding value, you are giving him every opportunity to be seen by the people who enjoy these activities, be it showing, combined driving, parades, or anything else you can think of.

The Importance of Photos

With any advertising, whether online or print, photos are critical to the success of the ad. It's very difficult to get someone excited about the prospect of a new horse when they don't even know what he looks like. That being said, a bad photo is worse than no photo at all.

While a good photograph can make a horse look even better than he is, a bad photo does the opposite. Miniature Horses can be a challenge to photograph well, and too often photos are taken at angles that don't flatter them.

First, get your horse cleaned up. Don't feel you have to do a full show groom for sale photos (though you certainly can), but you will need to give him a good grooming and polish. You don't want a half-grown-out bridle path, muddy feet, or a mane full of wind knots. Make sure he's had a recent hoof trim and looks clean and healthy.

In the day of smart phones with good cameras attached, you don't need to invest in a camera for basic sale photos, and when a potential buyer requests video or additional photos, it is very straightforward to take and send media.

"Miniature Horses have HUGE personalities! They are more lovable than my 'big' horses. And they love human attention and interaction. My youngster will practically beg for me to put a halter on her and do groundwork. She whinnies every time I go out my back door, even if she is out grazing and no food is involved. She loves to follow me around and be involved in what I'm doing."

Dorothy Marsh

Get a helper to either take the photos for you, or handle the horse. A good place to start is to get a good full body side shot, and a nice photo of his head and neck. The trick to getting the two or three great photos you need is to take lots of photos, and since in the current age of digital photography, it is easy to take as many photos as you need. Just keep clicking away.

The biggest secret to taking a good photo of a Miniature Horse is to get low. Taking a photo when you are standing, looking down at the horse, is never going to be flattering. You will make his legs look shorter, and his head bigger. Get low, and get as far away as you can and still get a good photo. When using a camera with a zoom lens, get far enough away so you can zoom in, and it will improve your photo.

A third person as an "ear-getter" can be a great asset. Arm your "ear-getter" with a pail filled with treats, noise makers, stuffed animals, anything that will get your horse's attention, to get a moment of great neck position, arch, and expression to show him off to his best advantage. When you don't have a third person, your horse handler can double as ear-getter, but it usually works best with teamwork.

Always be aware of the background of your photos. You don't want to take them with the poopiest corner of the pasture in view, or the bit of fence that's falling down, and you should also choose an uncluttered background so that the horse doesn't have a fencepost or tree growing awkwardly out of his head or back. Sometimes it's best when you can put the horse at the top of a rise and yourself at the bottom, so you can shoot with sky or horizon behind him.

Have no help? Take a couple with the horse standing tied to a nice fence. Or, the most

flattering photos you are likely to get on your own will be at liberty. Keeping your horse in the barn or a small pen overnight, then turning him out to play in a pasture with a pretty background gives you a chance to get some nice action shots (figs. 15.5 A & B).

Screening Potential Homes

One of the biggest challenges to selling a horse is simply parting with him. It can be very hard to see him leave for a new home, especially if you have any hesitation about the knowledge and dedication of the new owner. It can help to remember that you don't have to sell your horse to someone: if you have a bad feeling about the home for any reason at all, you can simply say, "I don't feel that you and this horse are a good match, but I wish you good luck in your search for the right horse."

Ask lots of questions of potential buyers, about their horse experience, their plans for this horse, and about the other horses they own. You are within your rights to request a reference from a vet

15.5 A & B Taking a bit of time when grooming and preparing, as well as learning the best angles to flatter your Miniature Horse, can make a big difference in the quality of your photos. Even if you're on your own, getting a photo of your horse in movement is always better than him grazing!

and farrier, and when a buyer is reluctant to share this information, perhaps it isn't the right home.

Think about the extensive questionnaires that dog breeders require before placing a puppy in a new home; if a buyer is offended by a few simple questions about the quality of care, that is likely not the right place for your horse. You need to be comfortable with the situation as well as the buyer.

You can also make up a sales contract that says the buyer will give you the first right of refusal should the horse be sold. This way, you are able to bring him home again and find his next home yourself so you can keep track of him. These contracts probably aren't going to legally guarantee that you will get the horse back, but they don't hurt, and can make sure your buyer knows that you are serious about doing everything you can to keep your horse in an appropriate home for his whole life (fig. 15.6).

A buyer may ask for a pre-purchase exam. While it can mean a bit of legwork on your part, handling a horse or hauling him to the veterinary clinic, it's a very good sign that you have a serious buyer and, most likely, a good home with a conscientious owner. The vet will examine your horse from head to toe, and perform a soundness exam, which will involve watching the horse move on a circle and in straight lines, as well as flexion tests to check for joint issues. The buyer pays for the exam, and, therefore, owns the information that is discovered, but if the deal doesn't come to pass, you can ask for details of the examination to be sent to you and your vet, giving you good information moving forward.

"Why do I like Miniature Horses? Intelligence per pound."

Jennifer Jacula

15.6 By answering all your buyer's questions and pairing her with the right horse for her needs, you'll have a happy buyer who will recommend you to others, and peace of mind knowing that your horse is in a good, long-term home. Sarah Walters with her first drive at home with her new horse, Slick.

Afterword

When I was 18 months old, in the fall of 1981, my grandparents, Merv and Claudia Giles, took a road trip to the eastern United States, and came home with three Miniature Horses. Bunny, Twinkles, and Champ were the start of our herd. A driving team of mares followed soon after, and I have photos of me "driving" the team at age two, with Grandad feeding cows off the back of the wagon.

Since then, there has never been a summer in my life that wasn't spent showing Miniature Horses. A lifelong horse learner, when I finished high school I went to Olds College and got a diploma in Equine Science then worked for seventeen years at an equine veterinary clinic. I'm an Equine Canada certified instructor, and I love working with horses and their people, as well as sharing and promoting Miniature Horses.

Whether I am reaching my goals with my performance horses, teaching someone the basics of harness fit, or just feeding my herd, lugging hay

The author with her grandad in 1981 with their first three Miniature Horses. The start of it all!

bales through the snow drifts of a Canadian winter, I will be forever grateful to my grandad and grandma for setting me on this path.

Miniature Horses bring me a lot of joy, and I hope that you find the same enjoyment with the Miniature Horses in your life.

Index